Yvonne Vaz Ezdani grew up in Burma, married and had two daughters there. The family repatriated to Goa in the early 1980s and she now lives in her paternal family home in Saligao, Goa. She was a teacher in a Higher Secondary School, with a master's degree in English literature from Rangoon University and an education degree from Annamalai University. She is now a school counsellor. Yvonne enjoys reading, writing and travelling to visit her daughters and their families.

NEW SONGS OF THE SURVIVORS
The Exodus of Indians from Burma

YVONNE VAZ EZDANI

SPEAKING
TIGER

SPEAKING TIGER PUBLISHING PVT. LTD
4381/4, Ansari Road, Daryaganj,
New Delhi–110002,
India

First published by Speaking Tiger in paperback 2016

Copyright © Yvonne Vaz Ezdani 2015
excerpt from *White Butterflies* by Colin McPhedran copyright © New South Publishing 2002
excerpts from *Bravo Mum* copyright © Shakuntala Peter 2004
Pages 217–219 are a continuation of this copyright page.

ISBN: 978-93-85755-21-7
eISBN: 978-93-85755-19-4

10 9 8 7 6 5 4 3 2 1

Typeset in Adobe Garamond Pro by SÜRYA, New Delhi
Printed at ....

An earlier version of this book was published as
Songs of the Survivors by Goa 1556 in 2007

All rights reserved.
No part of this publication may be reproduced,
transmitted, or stored in a retrieval system, in any form or
by any means, electronic, mechanical, photocopying,
recording or otherwise, without the
prior permission of the publisher.

This book is sold subject to the condition that it shall not,
by way of trade or otherwise, be lent, resold, hired out,
or otherwise circulated, without the publisher's
prior consent, in any form of binding or cover
other than that in which it is published.

*In memory of my parents,
Lucio Alexander and Lucy Vaz,
for sharing their stories and bringing alive for me
a time before my own.*

'Every life leaves behind an echo that is audible to those who take the trouble to listen.'
—Amitav Ghosh, *The Glass Palace*

Contents

Foreword
by Amitav Ghosh
xi

Introduction
1

PART I: GOAN VOICES

Chapter 1 In Times of Peace

Why, when and how Goans migrated to Burma – Memories of the community before war broke out
11

Chapter 2 23 December 1941

Rumours of war in British-ruled Burma – The Goan community in Rangoon was happily preparing for Christmas and did not heed warnings of a Japanese invasion
38

Chapter 3 10.10 am

The bombing of Rangoon took everyone by surprise – Survivors relate their personal experiences of that horrific morning
42

Chapter 4 Horror, Death and Destruction

Survivors remember the immediate aftermath of the bombing
47

Chapter 5 Thereafter: 24 December 1941–April 1942

Survivors recall days of fear and anxiety as bombings continue
54

Chapter 6 We Have to Flee

The exodus begins - Nightmare escapes by plane and ship - Many were denied berths and seats and families were torn apart

73

Chapter 7 The Great Trek

Some survivors walked to India - Crossing high mountains, thick forests and swollen rivers - Hunger, disease and other perils

88

Chapter 8 Surviving Japanese Rule in Burma

Stories of life under Japanese occupation in Burma

108

Chapter 9 Refugees in India

Condition of refugees who had fled Burma - Rehabilitation in India - Role of the British government - Refugee camps

129

Chapter 10 Return to Burma—A Historical Perspective

After the British recaptured Burma - Rebuilding lives in Burma

137

Chapter 11 Postscript—A Granddaughter's Story

150

PART II: OTHER VOICES

Chapter 1 An Excerpt from *White Butterflies* by Colin McPhedran

An account of the bombing of Myitkyina airport—the last functioning airport in Burma

159

Chapter 2 Helen the Legend and Jerry the Writer

Author and poet Jerry Pinto interweaves fragments of a personal family story into the story of Helen, the legendary Bollywood dancer

165

Chapter 3 Benegal Dinker Rao: Barefoot from Burma to India, 1942

Benegal Dinker Rao's story of the trek, as written by his nephew Arvind Benegal

171

Chapter 4 Shakuntala's Story

Shakuntala Peter gives a detailed account of her family trapped in Burma during the Japanese occupation

178

Chapter 5 Bravo Mum

The experiences of the brave and strong Daisy David Ramalingam, by her daughter, Shakuntala Peter, as she reunited her family in Burma

188

Chapter 6 My Memoirs—Gerry O'Connor

Gerry O'Connor, an Anglo-Indian lady, tells of the effects of the War, the trek to India and life in Burma

197

Chapter 7 War-time Memoirs—M.P. Vedachalam

M.P. Vedachalam brings out the discrimination faced by Indians who were forced to trek on the more difficult 'black route'

201

Acknowledgements
214

Photo Credits
217

Bibliography
220

Foreword

To write about the Indian past is almost inevitably to be confronted with a disheartening paucity of source material. I had to face this problem in a particularly acute form while writing about the 1942 exodus from Burma in my novel, *The Glass Palace*. Such documentation as I was able to find was overwhelmingly of British provenance; accounts written by Indians and other Asians were pitifully few even though they were by far the most numerous amongst the hundreds of thousands of people who left Burma at that time.

In his article 'A Forgotten Long March' the historian Hugh Tinker writes: 'Because the thousands on the march included every section of the Indian community in Burma one might have supposed that some among them—teachers, writers, social workers perhaps—would have recorded their memories of the experience. Perhaps some did: but it has not been possible to trace any such personal account. For most, it was an experience they wanted to forget: and who anyway was interested in reading their experiences? They were not heroes: either to other Indians or to the Burmese or the British.'*

---

*Hugh Tinker, 'A Forgotten Long March: The Indian Exodus from Burma, 1941' *Journal of South East Asian Studies*, 7/1, March 1975.

Fortunately the situation is not quite as dire as Tinker's observations suggest. Over the years I have heard reports of books and magazine articles in a number of Indian languages including Bengali, Assamese and Tamil: a systematic search would probably bring many such to light. Some other accounts, written for family consumption, have also begun to surface of late—and it is a matter of great pride for me that my website has played a part in this. Several survivors, and members of their families, have written to me about the exodus; a memoir written by a participant, Captain Nadir S. Tyabji—a truly remarkable document—has also appeared as a series of posts on my blog.

But there can be no doubt that a very promising body of material remains as yet largely untapped: human memory. At this point in time, seventy-two years after the event, the number of remaining survivors is very small. But many stories have been passed on within their families and it is of the utmost importance that these be preserved.

With every passing year the urgency of creating a written and accessible record grows ever more pressing: this indeed is why Yvonne Vaz Ezdani's *New Songs of the Survivors*—based on the memories of Burma's once-thriving Goan community—is so important. It is, so far as I know, the first attempt to write an oral history of the 'Forgotten Long March' drawing on the recollections of survivors and their descendants. Indeed the book is much more than an oral history: the manner of its telling is such as to allow the reader to witness the events as they unfold, giving the narrative the vividness and momentum of a novel. It is a remarkable and innovative account and deserves to find a large readership.

Amitav Ghosh
December 30, 2014

Introduction

This book began with a series of stories that my father, Lucio Alexander Vaz, would tell me. There were some moments so startling in their ability to conjure up pictures that I have not forgotten them. 'And on that long, difficult walk from Burma to India, some people became so weak with hunger that they did not even have the strength to pull out grass from the ground to eat. Instead they had to lie down and eat the grass off the ground like cattle,' my father would say, his voice full of awe at such determination to live.

This did not seem like the Burma I knew. As a young girl growing up in independent Burma, we sang the Burmese anthem at school every day, belting out '*Da doe pyay, da doe myay, doe paing de myay*' (This is our country, this is our land, we own this land). This particular line would sometimes take me back to stories I had heard about 'British days', 'Japanese occupation', wars and bombings. This country, this land, was once upon a time ruled by wealthy, powerful Burmese kings, but what did that matter when ranged against the muskets of the white man and his determination to plunder the riches of the country, its teak and rice and rubies, and later, oil? Burma was conquered by the British after three Anglo-Burmese Wars (between 1824 and 1886) and governed from afar by the Queen of England. During the Second World War, it suffered violent conflicts, great destruction and the deaths of thousands of innocent people, beginning in 1941. Then the Japanese Emperor and his soldiers became the 'masters'. About three years later, the British returned and drove the Japanese out. Burma finally became a free nation in January 1948.

When I began to write this book, I sought others who would corroborate my father's story because it was so disturbing. I offer it here as the catalyst for this book, this enterprise: the image of an Indian in some dark jungle, lying on the ground in such a state of exhaustion that he would nibble grass in order to survive.

I realised that other people had other catalysts. Here is Jerry Pinto's version of the Burmese story from his award-winning novel, *Em and the Big Hoom*. The unnamed narrator is on his own quest. He wants to understand how his mother had a 'nervous breakdown', but Burma comes into her story too.

> But each time Em told me something about her life, I would examine it for signs, for early indications of the 'nervous breakdown'. It was almost an obsession and might have something to do with my curiosity about her life. She was born in Rangoon, I knew and had come to India on one of the ships that crossed the Bay of Bengal when the Japanese attacked Burma. Her father had walked, from Rangoon to Assam; legend had it that he had departed with a head of black hair and appeared again in Calcutta with a shock of white hair. Was this it? Was this the break? She didn't seem to remember much about that crossing except how she used orange sweets to quell her nausea and had begun menstruating on board the ship. Was this just how

Introduction

people remembered things, in patches and in images, or was this the repression of a painful memory?

Somewhere along the way their piano had been jettisoned to lighten the boat. When I first heard this, I thought it was a good place for things to start, for my mother's breakdown to begin. I imagined the dabbassh as the piano hit the water and perhaps a wail of notes. I imagined my mother weeping for the piano as it began to bubble its way to the bottom of the Bay of Bengal. I cut between her tears, the white handkerchief handed to her by her impatient mother, the plume of seabed dust, the tearsoaked face, the first curious fish…

Then I heard another Roman Catholic Goan family tell of their piano. And another. And a fourth. Then I got it. The pianos were a metaphor, a tribal way of expressing loss. It did not matter if the pianos were real or had never existed. The story was their farewell to Rangoon. It expressed also their sense of being exiled home to Goa to a poor present. The past could be reinvented. It could be rich with Burmese silk and coal mines and rubies and emeralds and jade. It could be filled with anything you wanted and a piano that was thrown overboard could express so much more than talking about how one lent money out at interest in the city. Or how one taught English to fill up the gaps of a school-teacher's salary.

These were common stories to us children. We had heard of so many Indians who lived in Burma and had been forced to give up everything they had worked for and earned: their homes and cars, their businesses and shops, their lives even, and flee to India after the Japanese invasion and aerial bombardment in 1941–42. In my family, these stories acquired a particular potency because the bombs had come so close. During the Second World War, my grandparents, parents and uncles lost their home and everything they had in April 1942, during the first aerial bombing of Taunggyi in the Southern Shan State of Burma. They went through great physical and mental suffering but survived in Japanese-occupied Burma, only leaving for India much after the Second World War, in the 1960s. (Their story is told in detail in Chapter Eight of this book.)

Among those who succeeded in fleeing to India, the lucky ones flew home. Others followed by ship, crossing the Bay of Bengal under the constant threat of bombardment. And then there were those who walked, who made the long march from Burma to India, all the way to Manipur and then Assam, where they caught trains and slowly made their way home. Some had to walk the more hazardous route further north across the Hukaung Valley which came to be called the Valley of Death. Evacuees from the south escaped to Chittagong via Cox Bazaar. Finally, there were those who stayed in Burma. They must have assumed that, in the same way as the British had colonised Burma, the Japanese were just another coloniser of another colour. But they would carry the physical and psychological scars of this experience for decades. They often told of those dark days, the horror and the hardships they faced, and how they lived in fear of the Japanese soldiers.

I need to add here that the stories were distressing in a certain way: they were about life-and-death situations, wars and bombs, soldiers and enemies. My mother, Lucy, told me of how she was stalked by some Japanese soldiers who wanted to put her away in a camp where rape and torture were rampant. She was young, attractive, terrified and resolved to consume a bottle of Tincture of Iodine—even those words today seem to have an Olde Worlde ring to them—to end her life rather than suffer the cruelties that the Japanese soldiers of that time were known to inflict on their prisoners of war. The day they came to arrest her, a friend of the family who was an English-Japanese interpreter happened to accompany them and his gift of the gab as well as my grandmother's offer of fresh strawberries and cream helped change their minds and they left my mother alone after that.

In the safety of Goa in the 1980s, another country, another world, another era when the Axis powers were now history's bogeymen, these incidents took on a slightly unreal air. They were stories; not the standard-issue bedtime stories to be sure, but since my parents had both survived, they seemed to have the air of a happy ending.

After we repatriated to Goa, I was always on the look-out for stories from survivors of the Anglo-Japanese war in Burma. As anyone who pays attention to the life cycle of a story will tell you, time is the ever-present enemy. Many factual stories remain only in the oral tradition; they are passed from generation to generation and each telling distorts them a little, a game of Burmese whispers if you wish. Some simply die with the passing of those who lived through them. And so, I began making rough notes of the stories I was told.

Then, in the late 1990s, Thelma Menezes came into the picture. She was a strong, beautiful, half-Burmese lady, bedridden and in constant pain, but well known as a freelance columnist for the Pune dailies. She was one of the survivors of the trek across the Indo–Burma border in 1942 and spoke often of her experiences. When I remarked that the stories of the survivors of the Second World War in Burma should be recorded for posterity, she told me that I could do it. I wanted to tell the untold stories but writing a book seemed like a distant dream. The seeds of *Songs of the Survivors* were sown then but at least two years must have passed before I dared to think about it again.

I realised that most people in India had no idea of the incredible accounts of extreme hardship faced with so much courage and resilience. *Songs of the Survivors* was born out of this desire to share the oral, first-hand accounts that I had collected over the years. I happened to mention it to Frederick Noronha, a journalist and friend, who was cycling down the lane in front of my house and had stopped by to chat. He encouraged me to start on the project. In 2006, I began writing down the individual stories, with no real blueprint for the book. Thelma got me four contacts who added their stories to the ten my relatives and friends had contributed. I also tried to get more contacts, mainly Goans, to write about their war-time experiences in Burma. As a result of an appeal sent out on Goanet*, we were able to get four more narratives. While I was putting together the book, five more survivors came to know of the project through word of mouth and I was happy to include their stories. I do not seem to have started a moment too soon. Eleven of the survivors who contributed their experiences have since passed away.

With encouragement and support from Frederick Noronha, publisher of Goa 1556, *Songs of the Survivors* was released in December 2007.

---

*A network started in 1994 by Herman Carneiro in Boston at http://lists.goanet.org

Introduction

When a second edition was being planned, I decided to make substantial changes. Part I of this edition focuses on the stories of Burma-Goans. I wanted to avoid the repetitions that arose because the contributors were people of the same community relating the same events, so the individual stories from the original *Songs of the Survivors* have been reframed into one narrative, with different chapters for specific dates, events and themes. Part II gives a different perspective of the exodus from Burma by focussing on the experiences of non-Goans. I have included three new accounts of the trek, the trauma of families trapped in Burma during the Japanese occupation, an excerpt from Colin McPhedran's *White Butterflies* and a piece by Jerry Pinto.

While recapturing the memories of a generation that is advancing in age, *New Songs of the Survivors* also seeks to record little-known tales of determination and survival that are relevant not only to that period of history in Burma and India, but to the human spirit everywhere.

Yvonne Vaz Ezdani,
Goa, 2014

PART I: GOAN VOICES

Chapter 1

In Times of Peace

All things being equal, you would rather stay at home.
But things are rarely equal and so those who have studied migration talk about there being a 'push factor' and a 'pull factor'. In the case of many of the Goans who went to Burma in the late eighteenth century and the early nineteenth century, there mustn't have been too much of a push factor, unless you count the terminal decline of the Portuguese empire and its complete lack of interest in the economic development of its colony, Goa. On the other hand, Bombay beckoned from just a few hundred kilometres to the north, pulsating with electricity and energy, home to the mills and the docks and the ships on which a bright Goan boy might make his fortune. There were jobs to be had and rupees to be repatriated.

These days, at a time when a trip to Goa is de rigueur for most Indians, it might be interesting to note that back then, you would have had to have a passport to move from Goa to Bombay. You would be moving from the Portuguese Estado da India to the British Colonial Empire of India—Queen Victoria took over from the East India Company in the aftermath of the first war of independence in 1857.

But once the Goan boy had made the change, he had a range of choices. If he managed to get into the railways, he could end up anywhere on the subcontinent's iron circulatory system. If he was looking for work in business or other services, he could stay in Bombay, comfortingly close to home, or he could range further afield to Calcutta or to Delhi or Lucknow or Lahore. He could sail to the British or Portuguese colonies in East Africa.

Or he could go to Rangoon.

For, in 1885, Burma became a province of the British Empire. The Goans who ventured there were perhaps beguiled by the tales of its wealth, as were so many Indians from other parts of the country. They had been told the standard stories of an enchanting and prosperous country, the easy availability of jobs and the conviviality of the community that would meet them. Perhaps they felt that Bombay and Calcutta were already too crowded. Perhaps they had family in Burma, or a friend who wrote letters home.

Burma was known as a rich and fertile land and it was generally felt that there were fortunes to be made there, in rice and in teak, in rubies and in coal and, later, in oil. Even if a fortune wasn't sought, the possibility of a job in all the allied industries and support mechanisms attracted a steady stream of Indians who migrated there as civil servants, soldiers, river pilots, labourers, traders, etc. The influx of migrant Chinese and Indians filled cities like Rangoon and Moulmein, which became bustling commercial hubs.

Rangoon was the commercial and political capital of Burma. John L. Christian in his book, *Burma,* writes,

'Moghul Street which was Rangoon's Wall Street, presented a striking scene during business hours. Thousands of prosperous merchants and their clerks, principally Hindus dressed in Ghandi [sic] caps and homespun, thronged the street, conducting much of their business in the open air.' He describes pre-war Rangoon as 'a city of electric lights, paved streets, cinemas and night spots with gaudy neon signs.'

It was known as the most cosmopolitan city in Southeast Asia. From the mid-nineteenth century onwards it was never truly a Burmese city. Till the Second World War broke out, it had more foreigners than Burmese residents. 'Armenians, Japanese, Persians, Arabs, Jews and a motley of other Europeans besides multitudes of Indians and Chinese all found a ready home in Burma,' observed Christian.

Food was plentiful. It was said that in Burma, 'The farmer tickles the soil and it laughs forth an abundant harvest'. Fertile land in the plains as well as in the cool hill regions produced a variety of cereals, fresh fruits and vegetables, while the long unpolluted coastline offered great quantities of fresh and preserved seafood and some of the world's loveliest pearls. Across the country there was an abundance of natural resources: rich petroleum oil-fields, forests of teak and pyinkado (a Burmese hardwood with a delicious maroon tinge), the imperial jade mines, the world's finest rubies and sapphires and other precious stones.

Household items were easily available and affordable; in other words, the economy was booming. Rowe & Co, the famous department store in Rangoon, was filled with European fashion, homeware, toys and select food items. It was housed in one of the largest and most elegant colonial buildings. The wide roads of Rangoon were lined with many such buildings, built by colonial architects who mixed the latest European styles with Oriental influences.

Most survivors who were forced to flee from Burma during the Second World War look back with nostalgia at those idyllic days, the carefree social whirl of parties and picnics, playing the piano and singing popular songs. One survivor relates that his parents' wedding celebrations lasted a full week.

Rangoon-Goans socialised with one another for the most part. It did not matter that they were not allowed to be members of the British Gymkhana Club as they had their own 'Portuguese Club'. Albert deSouza, who was just eleven years old when the war broke out, remembers it as 'the Anglo-Portuguese Club, where families met for social occasions, like parties, dances, sporting events, etc. Many young men and women made their debut in Goan society in the congenial atmosphere of this social club situated on the upper floor of one of the buildings on Sparks Street. Those who wished to be "seen" by Goan society would naturally make it a point to be a habitué of this club,' Albert recalls.

Rags-to-riches stories were common among Goans and others. They were able to give their children an excellent education at the missionary schools and to raise their status in life. The businesses that some of them established, flourished. An aristocratic Goan family, the D'Souzas, founded E.M. D'Souza, one of the largest pharmaceutical houses in Burma, which continued to prosper even after Burma gained independence.

Albert deSouza's maternal grandfather, Gasper Pereira,

had first migrated to Burma in the early twentieth century, and he and his wife worked in the hotel business. Albert's parents, Anthony Xavier and Mary deSouza, owned the famous Albert Restaurant. He says, 'Our customers were from different walks of life. They were businessmen, engineers, seafarers, singles, and families too. It was an arduous job for my parents to be on their toes from early morning till midnight. Sometimes my brother and I helped when the rush was more and we had finished with school or were on a holiday. My father was a tough burly man who could take on any miscreants who needed disciplining. Some men got unruly after downing a few drinks and had to be silenced. We were famous for our vindaloo, a Goan dish.'

Life in pre-war Burma was not just about amassing material wealth. The old Buddhist monasteries, the magnificent Shwe Dagon Pagoda and the innumerable white-washed or gilded pagodas crowning a thousand hills and nestling in valleys across the country created an aura of tranquillity over the land. Christian churches, Armenian churches, Hindu temples, mosques and synagogues could be found in almost every town or city and religion was an essential part of the lifestyle in Burma.

Goans were happy to attend church services and sustain the faith they had practised back home. The churches were also focal points of meeting with other members of their community and with their Indian, Anglo-Indian and Anglo-Burmese friends. Albert deSouza recalls that life was centred around the church. 'Our place of worship was a massive and grand cathedral with twin spires and built in Gothic style. People visiting St. Mary's Cathedral for the first time are awed by its size and magnificent architecture. I am told it resembled many of the cathedrals in Europe,' he says with pride.

Although most of the Goans who migrated to Burma were not highly educated or skilled, except perhaps in music or cooking, they seem to have succeeded in whatever jobs they found or businesses they set up. Many Goans held Portuguese passports. They were Christians who wore European clothes and spoke English. So Burma-Goans took on a distinct identity. They acquired not only wealth, but worked with sincerity and great capability in responsible posts and established a respected and unique community. That the British valued their services is evident from their promotions and prestigious positions in government departments.

One such was Anthony John D'Cruz of Cruz Vaddo Saligao, who left Goa at the age of seventeen. He was carrying his precious violin when he boarded a ship to Rangoon to make his fortune as a musician. In Rangoon, he attracted the attention of the Presidency Postmaster, whose son took violin lessons from him. This Englishman gave AJ, as he was known, his first job in the postal department as an unpaid probationer. The diligent, determined young AJ educated himself and gradually rose in rank to become Acting Presidency Postmaster of Lucknow, India, earning a four-figure salary, which in those days was a fabulous sum.

Burma must have meant something to AJ for, after his retirement, he chose to go back there to build a mansion and live in luxury. One of his sons became a doctor and in the course of time rose to be Assistant Director of Medical Services Burma, another son became a Forest Officer, the next a school headmaster and the other three children did well for themselves too. The grandchildren were getting a good education when the Japanese bombings of Rangoon took place and the family had to flee to India. All this, and the other material that I have used to reconstruct his story came to me from AJ's granddaughter, Patsy Menezes, who sent me an account written by AJ along with a few pages from his diary of the trek back to India.

The late Donald Menezes, AJ's grandson, was studying in Rangoon University when the war broke out. He recorded his wartime experiences in an article, 'Tragedy in Rangoon and the Great Burma Trek' (published in *Je Me Souviens*, a special publication of the Canorient Christian Association of Toronto, Canada) excerpts of which are included in this book.

A variety of stories about the lives of Burma-Goans in peacetime took various routes to come to me. The following sections chart the backgrounds of the survivors whose experiences are related in the rest of this book

*

AJ had taken some other young Saligaonkars to Burma, such as his neighbour, Jose Francis Saldanha, who became a Customs Officer and brought up a large family there. His daughter, Sylvia D'Gama, told me that her father's job took the family to various coastal towns and she and her five siblings enjoyed the variety of seafood and delicious Burmese cuisine. They were living in Rangoon when the city was bombed.

*

I first met Maurice Machado who had also lived in Burma. Maurice felt that his cousin, Tony Machado, would be able to tell me more than he could. Tony lives most of the time in Mumbai but has a holiday home in Saligao, Goa and it was a pleasure to meet him personally. His encounter with Burma begins with his father, Maxy Machado, an orphan with hardly any education and no finances who was taken to Burma by his step-uncle in 1909.

When the war broke out in 1941 he had become the station master of a major railway station. Tony Machado recalls, 'Dad had no recollection of his parents, as he had been orphaned as a toddler and raised by his widowed maternal aunt. In these difficult circumstances, he spent his childhood in Goa, working in the fields alongside his aunt, growing paddy and beans, instead of going to school. His education was therefore sketchy and he assumed that he could only be employed at a low level in Burma—and that too because of the special status enjoyed by Anglo-Indians, an identity Goans often claimed as well.

'I was not yet eleven years old when we left Burma, but, as I recall, we were prosperous. My father's hard work and sober habits enabled him to save enough to invest in sugarcane plantations which supplemented his income. Furthermore, he would rear poultry in the backyard of our sprawling railway quarters. "Kitchen waste is fowl's luxury," was his famous dictum. An average of one hundred and fifty birds was normal, so fresh eggs and chicken were had for the asking anytime. At the time of our flight from Burma, Dad was the station master of Pyinmana, a major rail junction in Central Burma. It was doubtless through meritorious and dedicated service that he had risen to this responsible position.

'Mom, Matilda (née de San Lazaro) was an equally capable and accomplished lady of the house and she was assisted by a retinue of servants. Besides the coolie and butler, there were maids and valets, all resident in the servants' quarters. She had her own social circle with parties and outings. She was also well-connected with the clergy and sisters, so it was common for the visiting priests and even bishops to reside with us. They were mostly English, Irish or Italian visiting clergy.'

Even after so many decades, Tony still has vivid memories of the country he left as a ten-year-old. He remembers 'a rich country; nature has been bountiful with lush vegetation and dense forests of teak and pyinkado covering the countryside. Besides, there is valuable mineral wealth, oil, rubies and other precious stones, most of which is unexplored. The Burmese are a contented happy lot, affable and hospitable. A bowl of plain weak tea is invariably offered on a casual visit. The men are easy going and leisure loving. It is a common sight to see young men playing chinlon, a Burmese game, involving a wicker ball tossed in the air with the feet by ten men in a circle, in the golden hours of the morning. Older men would sit and watch with their cheroots or fat cigars puffing to glory. The women are industrious, both in the kitchens and in the fields, which produce abundant harvests. The monsoon rains fed the fields and so did the Irrawaddy, which runs through the whole country, facilitating irrigation where needed.'

*

Felicity Fernandes' parents were close friends of my grandparents and I was happy to receive a written account of her memories as well as some rare and interesting photographs from her. Felicity observes that, about a century ago, when most people were travelling westward towards greener pastures, her father, Frank Rodrigues, decided to do just the opposite. Leaving his humble home in Ribander in the Tiswadi sub-district of Goa, on the scenic banks of the Mandovi river, he travelled eastward to make his fortune in the mysterious and beautiful country of golden pagodas, precious jade, teakwood and elephants.

She adds, 'He was about twenty-five years old, but he was a mature young man who had the responsibility of looking after a younger brother, and a cousin, who was partially blind. By dint of hard work and with the help of friends, especially the late Luis Joseph and Natividade Vaz, Goans who were well settled in Taunggyi, he started his own business in Kalaw, a lovely little hill station in the Southern Shan State. He named the store after himself, Frank Rodrigues, and the picture in Dad's album clearly proclaims that he dealt in the sale of oil, wines and general merchandise, including Polson's Butter and Coffee. His brother followed him to Burma soon thereafter and settled in Rangoon, where he was employed in a well-known pharmaceutical company owned by a Goan, E.M. D'Souza.

Dad's shop was on the ground floor and we lived just above. We had a dog named Nero, and only one neighbour, a Japanese doctor and his family. They were reserved but very helpful. Though Dad and Mum lived in Kalaw for about ten years only, they had made many good friends who would gather in the shop in the evenings and discuss the growing tension in the world and how it would affect them. Whilst the men talked politics below, the womenfolk would come up and have coffee with Mum. Among them was a Miss Crescent, an Englishwoman, who was a nurse and a close friend; when my brother was born in July 1941, he was named Crescent after her. We were very happy in Kalaw but were compelled to return to India when the Japanese began bombing Burma.'

*

Father Coleman D'Souza, SJ*, put me in contact with his brother, Gerald D'Souza, who passed away in 2014 in Mumbai. Gerald had shown an interest in his father's stories about his time in Burma and also did a lot of research on the period of Japanese rule in Burma. He sent me his detailed, well-written account and I learned many new facts, especially about the Indian National Army's activities in Burma and the functioning of the Burmese, British and Japanese governments.

Gerald D'Souza writes, 'My grandfather, Alex de Souza, from the village of Sangolda in the sub-district of Bardez in Goa, was a typical early emigrant to Burma. He had studied Portuguese, Konkani, Christian doctrine and sacred music, besides the violin, at his parish school in Sangolda. This was the era of silent movies, when live musicians with excellent sight-reading skills were needed to provide the background music to films from printed scores provided by the producers. Musicians were also needed for the orchestras in hotels and clubs and in the British military bands. Talented Goan musicians found ready opportunities in the large cities of British India, of which Burma was then a province.

'In Rangoon, Alex lived in a chummery (bachelors'

---

*Society of Jesus

lodgings) to begin with. He joined a string quartet of violins, viola and cello, playing light chamber music like Strauss waltzes, Hungarian dances, Gypsy airs, Italian ballads (cancions), Iberian tangos and the like for formal luncheons and dinners at the Strand Hotel and Pegu Club. He soon got more lucrative opportunities to play background music for silent films in larger orchestras at the Excelsior and other movie theatres in Rangoon.

'Alex encountered another De Souza family who were well-off and much Anglicized. They, with their four stylish and well-educated daughters, resided in the Indian upper-class Bauktaw suburb of the city. The De Souzas also owned a holiday home in Kalaw, a lovely hill-station perched at 4,600 feet on the western rim of the Shan plateau, where they would retire to every sweltering Burmese summer. Mary was one of the four daughters and Alex fell in love with her. She was willing to marry him provided he got a 'steady' job (meaning an office job, preferably with the government). And so that is what he set out to do, systematically, with real determination and grit. To improve his command over the English language, a pre-requisite for such an appointment, Alex spent all his spare time working his way through primers, books of grammar and composition, then stories for children by Hans Christian Anderson, and progressing to Rudyard Kipling, Charles Dickens and Thomas Hardy. He was eventually successful in getting appointed as a proof-reader in the Government Printing Press in Rangoon and married Mary soon after. He continued with selective musical engagements, which did not interfere with the job and eventually rose to the post of Examiner-in-Charge of the Press.'

Gerald continues, 'Mary and Alex had three children, named Martin (who would become my father in good time), Michael and Margaret. All of them had the benefit of a Baptist Missionary School secondary education in Rangoon, side by side with musical studies. Margaret qualified as a piano-teacher by acquiring a Licentiate Diploma of the Trinity College of Music (LTCM). Michael could play violin and double-bass, but made pharmacy his profession and eventually became a partner in the pharmaceutical firm of E. M. D'Souza & Co., Rangoon. Martin played the piano, but with an interest mainly in popular dance music, particularly in the balladic style popularised by Charlie Kunze. He developed a special affinity for, and fluency in, the music of George Gershwin, Hoagy Carmichael, Irving Berlin and Cole Porter, though he also loved to play the classical works of Chopin for his own pleasure, often late into the night, which helped to develop his technical mastery over the keyboard.

'Alex's entire family visited Goa for the decennial exposition of the incorrupt body of St. Francis Xavier between December 3, 1931 and January 10, 1932. That year, the Patriarch, D. Teotonio Manuel Ribeiro Viera de Castro, had invited all the ecclesiastical hierarchy of India, Burma, Ceylon and Japan for the occasion and more than 500,000 attended from these dioceses. Instead of returning to Burma with the rest of the family, Martin joined a band from Goa, which undertook seasonal contracts to play dance-music in the night-clubs of Bombay and Delhi.

'In 1934, Martin married Florence (Florie) Luis from Candolim. Five years later in September 1939, Florie was seven months pregnant, when Martin decided to take his little family to Burma, having decided to make his home in the hill-station of Maymyo, located 42 miles from Mandalay. Maymyo was the official summer capital of the government—Burma's answer to India's Simla, so to speak. Indian and Chinese traders were drawn to the town. Lining the Circular Road, they put up shops in rows of single-storey, timbered houses, with red-painted corrugated iron roofs. Retired Gurkha troops became drivers of gharries—colourful carriages, painted and designed almost like stagecoaches out of the Wild West—while their families settled in the surrounding villages provided willing hands to cultivate and crop pineapples, strawberries, litchis, avocados and all kinds of European vegetables, as well as coffee and bananas, which became abundantly available in the markets of Maymyo.

'Maymyo was highly developed, with an 18-hole (par 72) golf course and a magnificent 432-acre botanical garden set beside the largest lake. There were also several schools, mission hospitals, churches, and clubs, as well as hotels, inns and lodges catering to the annual summer influx of visitors. There were probably around 25,000 residents in Maymyo in 1939, the year Martin and his family headed there from Goa.

'After the train journey from Vasco da Gama in Goa through Castlerock to Londa and another longer one across the Deccan to Madras, the rough sea-voyage to Rangoon was a little too much for Florie, it seemed. She delivered a premature child (me) on the open seas between Madras and Port Blair, in the Andaman and Nicobar Islands. But we eventually settled in Maymyo.'

Gerald then warms to his tale of life in Burma. 'Apart from playing the pipe-organ in the church, Martin soon formed his own quintet with piano, bass, drums, trumpet and saxophone or clarinet. Its very first regular assignment was to play on weekends at the Candacraig Hotel, which was built in 1905, principally as a summer resort and relaxation centre for the staff of the Bombay-Burma Trading Company, but over the years become a popular, though elite, hotel. It was a fine red-brick beamed building, in the style of an English country house surrounded by pine trees, poplars, oaks, eucalyptus, chestnut and mahonia trees and brilliantly coloured rhododendron bushes. It offered many of the niceties: English food, early-morning tea and a lounge with a bar and a big fireplace for cold evenings. Martin also played in other clubs and halls for regular weddings, dances and balls, generally held during the summer when the hill-station would be bustling with people seeking refuge from the heat of the Burmese plains.'

*

Geraldine D'Souza's father, Tome Piedade Pinto, first went to Burma with a friend, Mr Castelino. She says, 'He settled in Rangoon and worked in Vienna Café, (bakers, confectioners and caterers). He then brought my mother and eldest brother, Anthony, from Goa. After some time, he gave up working for Vienna Café and started his own business, called Burma Café. It was situated on Phayre Street, which was a very long street that began on one side with the railway station and ended at the docks. We lived on 37th Street. We were a big family of four boys and four girls. The eldest, Anthony, joined the P&O liner and sailed to England and on their way back to Burma, they were torpedoed by a German submarine. Luckily they survived. When Anthony arrived back in Rangoon, he helped out in my father's business and later on joined the Royal Medical Army Corps.'

*

Isabelle Vaz, popularly known as Isa, is my aunt by marriage. Her father, Anju D'Souza, first went to Burma in the early twentieth century with his uncle, Hipoll D'Souza (also known as Myingyan D'Souza). Anju opened a liquor shop in Meiktila and was also an agent for a life insurance company. This job took him all over Burma to places as far north as Bhamo and down south to Mergui. 'He met my mother Ivy D'Souza, a Burma-born Goan, at the Portuguese Club in Rangoon, fell in love and married her at St. Mary's Cathedral. I and my brother Aloysious both grew up in Rangoon,' says Isabelle.

*

When Patricia Duarte Van Camp heard of Frederick Noronha's appeal on the Goanet mailing list, she had her son, Martin Van Camp, who was also living in Belgium, take down her story from her sick bed, before she passed away in 2008. I am grateful to Martin for taking the time and trouble to record his mother's war-time experiences.

Patricia began with the story of her father, Armando Marcus Duarte, who was born in 1883 in Guirim, Goa. His father, Lourenço Caetano Duarte, was one of the many Goan pioneers who went to Karachi to try their hands at business ventures. Lourenço was one of the co-founders of the Indian/Ideal Life Assurance Company (ILACO) and one of the first sponsoring members of the Karachi Goan Association in 1892. So Patricia assumes that her father and his brothers grew up in Karachi and were educated there.

'In the beginning of the twentieth century, Armando went to Edinburgh to study medicine and in 1914 he graduated as MBChB (the equivalent of an MBBS). In 1917 he joined the Indian Medical Service. Within the next four to five years he joined the Egyptian Expeditionary Forces (EEF), and the 28th Punjabi Regiment in Palestine, Syria and Silicia. In April 1921, he returned to civilian life.

'Shortly after, he joined his uncle Joseph Celestino Duarte in Rangoon, Burma. Joseph Duarte was in charge of a dispensary and felt he could definitely use Armando's experience. Later on, Armando also worked in the Dufferin Hospital where he met his future wife, the Jewish doctor, Miss Rose Ramah Aaron, who was seventeen years younger than he. When they married in 1924, her father disowned her for marrying outside her faith.'

Patricia continues her story. 'When I was born, I was named Patricia Carmen Theresa and, as my mother had promised, I was baptised a Catholic. We lived on 49th Street in Rangoon. There was a kindergarten at the end of the street. It was a Protestant school. My primary and secondary school education was at the Branch Convent, an annex convent school run by Irish nuns. Our uniform was a white shirt, blue skirt and a blue tie.

'At the age of five, I got my first piano lessons. My parents and family noticed my talent for piano and I continued to take lessons from my godmother Queenie, who had an LTCL (Licentiate from the Trinity College) and later from Miss Eileen Strong. I was very impressed by this lady. She was extremely patient and confident in her work. She was a brilliant pianist and teacher. She saw my potential and I was the first of her pupils whom she entered for the "Exam Musicianship". At that time I was thirteen or fourteen years old. I had to give exams on "Transposition at Sight" and "Melody Making". I won a scholarship after these exams as I came first among the candidates in India, Burma and Ceylon.

'One of my first memories is when I was nearly four years old in 1929. My parents spoke with great respect and love about a man who was very humble and tried to uplift the poor. His name was Mahatma Gandhi. That day, my parents took me out and we were walking hand-in-hand, myself in the middle, through 49th Street and further on in the direction of the maidan (open field). The entire place was full of people; I had never ever seen such a huge crowd. In the middle of the maidan, he sat on a stage and spoke to the masses. Somehow we were able to get very close to Mahatma Gandhi and when he saw my parents and me he stood up and came to me and gently touched my cheek and said, "Do you love me, darling?" and "Will you always love me?" My mother wrote this down in her diary as she never wanted to forget this moment. Many years later I wanted to find out more and it seemed that Gandhi indeed was in Rangoon from March 8, 1929 until March 10, 1929. He addressed public meetings on March 8th and 9th and on March 10th he addressed meetings for Gujaratis, Arya Samajists, Indian gate-keepers, other Indians and students.

'Each day after school, I would go to a park near my home. Many children, younger and older than me, would come there and listen to my stories. I was famous for my concoctions. My dad introduced me to Francis Thompson and Edgar Allan Poe, P.G. Wodehouse and to Omar Kháyyám (his wonderful *Rubáiyát*). Perhaps that made me write short naïve poems later as a teen.

'When the Second World War broke out, it became clear

that our days in Rangoon were over. We had to look for a way to get out of the country.'

*

I met Lena Rego at the Home for the Aged in Old Goa. She struck me as a strong cheerful lady in spite of her many health problems. Her father, Casimir Rego, had been a driver in the Burma Railways. Originally from Assagao, North Goa, he had been taken to Singapore by his uncle and from there had moved to Burma as a young boy. He got his first job here as a fireman on the steam engines in the railways and later became a driver. On one of his visits to Goa, he married Julie Faria from Cunchelim and took her to Burma. He was transferred to places like Toungoo and Mandalay, but Lena grew up mainly in Rangoon and remembered the place very well. 'My mother busied herself taking care of her large family which included four daughters and three sons. We girls went to Good Shepherd Convent and my brothers studied at St. Paul's High School. We must have been well-to-do because there was good food, servants and other luxuries which we never lacked. We could also travel free on the trains and we often visited our Rego cousins in Moulmein.' Their house, the quarters allotted to them by the Burma Railways, was on Sparks Street.

*

Eric Menezes passed on in 2009. His many memories of pre-war Burma include some that made my mouth water. After a trip to Goa in 1939, he recalls the voyage back to Rangoon with his mother, escorted by a person named Gabru, a friend of Eric's father.

'It was a pleasant rail trip from Margao to Guntakal and then to Madras where we availed of the BI (British India

Steam Navigation) sailing to Rangoon the next day in the afternoon. It was quite windy and the sea rough, but to a young boy of eight it was fine. For a few hours the ship rolled and pitched quite a lot, so much so, that at times Mummy was confined to her cabin with sea sickness and I was the sole occupant of the dining room, with Gabru escorting. I always enjoyed my meals, the sea having whetted my appetite. I believe I went through the menu from soup to fruit salad with jelly and ice cream. Those days, travelling by second class was not demeaning at all and the cabin was quite comfortable. Gabru reported every day, and we roamed the ship. After a voyage of some three days, it was nice to see Rangoon again. One of the first landmarks one encounters is the golden spire of the Shwedagon pagoda, visible from the Rangoon Harbour. Daddy and the two servants were waiting at the jetty and then, of course, off to our home on 41st Street.

'Rangoon was a well-laid-out city on a grid pattern, with main thoroughfares and blocks of consecutively numbered streets in between. It was also modern with all amenities, including its famous Mughal Street and Chinatown. The Port Trust had fine gardens along the river front and beyond these were the steamer jetties on the Irrawaddy river. I was, of course, too young to remember everything as a grown up perhaps would, but I do recollect the Strand Hotel where my favourite treat was a small goblet of Maraschino cherries and Mummy's was an Italian-style cheese and tomato omelette (six eggs). Sometimes, in the late evenings, we would drive down to Mughal Street and be served with heavy snacks in the car itself. Since our car was an Austin convertible, it was a very simple matter to slide a narrow plank from one side to the other, whisk a table cloth and serve the food—hot, and, of course, very tasty. For some reason or the other, my helpings were usually preceded by a bowl of hot brain soup, but I do not think it improved my own grey cells in any special way. Visits to China Town were also an experience, with roaring fires and any variety of noodles or chow with fillings of chicken, pork, prawns, oysters—you name it—all served steaming hot and quite cheap. There was also one roadside Muslim eatery on the Sule Pagoda Road which specialised in egg paratha stuffed with mince and served with finely sliced onion and lime. My mouth still waters at the thought of it.

'I must not forget the individual food vendors, both Burmese and Chinese, food vendors who brought food and snacks literally to your doorstep. They used to carry their wares in covered baskets or wooden boxes balanced on both ends of a bamboo stave carried on their shoulders. Some were even provided with a fire in a brazier for a hot snack. If tempted, Mummy would sometimes buy a coconut-milk, jaggery syrup and sago refreshment nicely iced or a Chinese snack called corcodeo or something like that. Then there always was the popular Burmese Kaukswe and not forgetting the kulfi malai served right out of their sealed tin cones. But before I continue, a mention must be made of M.C. Pinto whose pastry and cake shop provided some really delicious products. The Silver Grill was a popular night spot which Mum and Dad went to sometimes; but this was strictly off limits for a young chap like me.

'I also have recollections of the main intersecting roads like Phayre Street, Dalhousie Street and of the Lady Dufferin Hospital where my younger brother was born in 1939. Yes,

Burma was a nice place, with very nice people richly endowed with natural resources including rice, teak, oil, gemstones and other valuable minerals and, with their simple lifestyles, the people lived comfortably.

'The Goan community may not have been large, but it was not too small either, mostly commercial or business and service oriented, with a sprinkling of teachers and musicians and possibly some doctors. It's now hard to remember the names of all the families my parents had contact with but I do remember the families of Anju D'Souza, his brother Jerry, Tony Sequeira, Balbino Athaide, Salvador Rodricks, the two Mandrick brothers, and the Silgardos. All somehow or the other made it back to India. "Visiting" and birthday bashes were the usual way of keeping contact, like perhaps anywhere else.

'Christmas was just a few days away. On 41st Street was the attractive Rowe & Co. I say "attractive" because it had a really lovely toy shop. Amongst the offerings for the Christmas of 1941, they had displayed a fine electric train set with a layout of tunnels, bridges, shunting yards and the works. Its price tag made sure that I did not get it, although Daddy was tempted. Instead, my Christmas present was a Hornby train set, spring-wound, with a largish circular track. I also got boxed lead soldiers, including the household cavalry and some models of tanks by Dinky toys. Unknown to us at that time, it was to be our last Christmas in Burma.'

*

Hugh Nazareth, who passed away in Bangalore in August 2015 at the ripe old age of 102 years, was a close family friend. His son, Noel, sent me the following account of life in pre-war Burma.

'Hugh's father Salvador Nazareth, of Candolim, Goa, used to travel by pathmari (sail boat) from Goa to Burma and trade coconuts, copra and coir rope for rice. On the last trip in 1901 their boat ran aground at Monkey Point, Rangoon, and was wrecked. So, when he went ashore to investigate, he found the possibility of settling in and doing business in Burma viable. He did not want to stay in Rangoon which was full of competitors and decided to go up country to Toungoo, about 170 miles from Rangoon, which was a fairly important district town. He bought a plot of land in a good location and built a house with a shop on the ground floor.

'He started business in Toungoo, made friends with the officers and got himself appointed as distributor for BOC (Burma Oil Company) petrol in Toungoo and the surrounding areas. As business increased he called his brother, Candido Nazareth, from Goa to join him and the business was called Nazareth Brothers.

'They expanded into medicines, learning some simple remedies which Salvador Nazareth used to compound, augmented by a range of imported patent medicines. He recruited a Portuguese doctor from Goa to help in this medicine business. This doctor made friends with the Government Civil Surgeon and their friendship greatly helped the medical business. Unfortunately, the Portuguese doctor had a fall and being unable to continue work, returned to Goa. Salvador appointed an Indian doctor to take his place. The latter worked with him for a couple of years and then left to set up his own medical practice.

'As part of their distributorship they needed transport, so they expanded into the transport business and their trucks used to ply to and from Rangoon and neighbouring towns. Being from an agricultural background, Salvador Nazareth acquired about ten acres of agricultural land on which he cultivated sugar cane. The sugar cane produced in his field did not measure up to a full wagon load, so he persuaded his neighbours to plant sugar cane and their joint produce was sent in wagon loads to Zeyawadi Sugar Factory, the largest sugar factory in Burma. Their own trucks proved useful to get the sugar cane to the railway wagon. They also set up a bakery and confectionery, since Toungoo was now a military base and had quite a high population of British officers and other ranks with their families. They produced up to 6,000 loaves of bread per day.

'They acquired the all-Burma distributorship for arms and ammunition, which they imported from manufacturers in England. These were supplied directly to the police and the army or sold in various shops in different parts of Burma and could be bought by individuals. There was no restriction on the sale of guns and ammunition to civilians.

'Hugh attended primary school in Toungoo, which by then had a convent, run by Italian Catholic nuns. He finished his schooling as a boarder at the Christian Brothers' school in Moulmein. He later graduated from Judson College in Rangoon.

Hugh's father died in 1935. His brother, Candido, had returned to Goa earlier in 1933. Hugh had to take over the running of the business, when they were having a really bad time because of the worldwide depression between 1933 and 1935. To increase his income during this depression, he worked as a collection agent of insurance premia on behalf of Oriental Insurance Co. This involved considerable travelling and thus fitted in with his distributorship businesses. He was also required to visit Rangoon frequently. Business began to pick up by 1939. Burma was unaffected by the war in Europe, until the Japanese bombed Rangoon in December 1941.'

*

Wilma Silgardo, whom I met at her home in Calangute, had lively memories of Burma. 'My father Cajetan Bernard Silgardo owned a shop—Silgardo & Co.—in Rangoon where he sold all kinds of musical instruments. He was also a piano tuner and never lacked work. He himself was a good musician who had trained in the violin in London. It is said that he was the first Goan to play the violin at the Albert Hall, London.' Wilma and her siblings were educated in India until 1937 and later in Burma. She recalls that the education system in Burma was much better then and the schools were well equipped, with swimming pools and skating rinks. It still amazed her that there was a piano in every classroom.

*

Although most Goans were of the opinion that, in general, the local people were good-natured and likeable, there was not much social interaction between the Burmese and foreigners living in Burma at that time.

Most Burmese in those days had little experience of the outside world. They seldom or never travelled abroad, but people from almost every land on the earth went to Burma. Burmese culture has traditionally been non-migratory, perhaps stemming from the fact that Burmese people were proud of and satisfied with their beautiful, wealthy country. They did not welcome the influx of people into their cities with open arms, but tolerated them, until later, when they realised that they were being gradually displaced from their ancestral land and that they had become mere onlookers at the new economic boom in their country. The British, Indians and Chinese profited during this period, but not the Burmese who, for some time, were not even conscious of being exploited. Later, when Burmese farmers became acutely aware that they were becoming landless strangers in their own land, because of the thousands of Indian labourers who were willing to work for less money, there was a sense that foreigners were becoming unwelcome.

Buddhism is a way of life for the Burmese and they are a society with deep spiritual values. Most Burmese people remain non-judgemental, non-materialistic and non-interfering in the lives of others. A saying goes that 'in schools of the west you learned how to make money but in the Burmese monastery school, a youth learned to be happy and contented.'

On the whole, the British regarded the Burmese with approval. Sir Clement Hindley, the first Chief Commissioner of Railways for India, described the Burmese in his address before the East India Association in London, as 'perhaps the most charming people in the whole of the British Empire'. James George Scott, who wrote under the Burmese pen name of Shwe Yoe, brought out with rare insight the fact that the Burmese were no inferior race. They could not be required to behave like Englishmen or any other people, but they had a wealth of customs and were tough and resilient on the one hand and, on the other, their insouciance, gracefulness of spirit and relaxed way of life made them unique and delightful. George Orwell was secretly all for the Burmese and against their oppressors, the British, even though he regarded the Burmese as an 'inferior' people. His essays reveal that he was annoyed at the resentment that some Burmese people openly showed him and other British officials.

Some Goans felt that resentment was sometimes directed at them too, when they were called 'kalas', a term of contempt for their dark skin, but they took it lightly. Albert deSouza seems to understand and says, 'Maybe we were too many, and were occupying their "space". We competed with them for jobs and took away their resources.' But in all probability, very few Goans must have realised that they were cooperating with the British and helping to enslave another country.

The good life ended abruptly. Peace was shattered on the morning of December 23, 1941 when the Japanese bombs fell. So many of these stories work their way through memory into massacre, as Burma was plunged into the Second World War. Soon after this began the exodus to India, which is said to be the largest mass migration in history.

Chapter 2

23 December 1941

It was a sunny day in the middle of the Second World War and fifteen days after the bombing of Pearl Harbour. All the schools in Rangoon were closed because of the threat of war coming to Burma. There were rumours of an air attack, so a watch was kept on the skies from Monkey Point, currently Myanmar's main naval facility, at Yangon.

About a week earlier, the Japanese had launched overland attacks on airfields in Tavoy and Mergui in Tenasserim near the Thai border in the south of Burma. The British were overwhelmed and forced to evacuate the town, but this did not make them less confident about their strength and ability to defend their colony—until the Japanese began air bombardments on Rangoon and, later, on other parts of the country.

The sections that follow are the personal observations and memories of survivors who experienced at first hand the Japanese bombing of Rangoon and the events that followed. At that time, most of them were children below the age of thirteen, living in Rangoon with their families. Eleven of them have now passed away.

*

Eric Menezes was only an eight-year-old when the attack began but he has a magnificent memory: 'Of course, rumours played their part and we were always being told that Japan was going to attack. But that is what the Japanese wanted, namely to strike terror into and demoralise the population. Europe had been at war since September 1, 1939. But till that day some two years later, it all seemed far away and there were no hardships or direct sufferings in India and Burma, where life continued as usual for the Goan expats too. Even though I was only eight years old at that time, I remember the general confidence that still prevailed. After all, Singapore was the impregnable bastion, and the Japanese adventure was certain to be beaten there by the British and American forces.'

But Eric's father had taken the precaution of moving his family out from the heart of Rangoon to a rented bungalow in a nearby suburb. 'Father would drive into town every morning to attend to his work. The only reminder of an expected war was the digging of a deep L-shaped trench in the garden. It had steps going down and a mud-covered roof, and was meant for use in case of an air raid. Life was quite comfortable at the Kokine Lake bungalow on the outskirts of Rangoon where we lived and we felt no anxiety. The government communiqués were guarded but not alarming, and people were advised not to keep too much cash at home to avoid robberies. So, life went on as normal, a little subdued perhaps, but there were no shortages of food or any other essential supplies.'

Everyone knew that war was coming but no one could really believe that the city would be bombed. Geraldine D'Souza (then Geraldine Pinto) remembers the trust they had in the

British. 'In November 1941, the Japanese had dropped leaflets asking the people to move out of Rangoon as they were going to give us a Christmas present. But the British said there was no need to fear as they were fortified with the Spitfire and Hurricane planes,' she recalls. 'No one really took heed of the Japanese when they announced over the radio on December 21, 1941 that they would soon be showering Rangoon with "Christmas toys",' concurrs Isabelle Vaz, who was just seven years old at the time and still Isa D'Souza.

Tony Machado, however, tells us that rumours and threats did have an effect on some people. 'The Japanese invasion of Burma was anticipated by the intelligentsia well before the first bombing on December 23, 1941. Hence, Rangoon was already partially evacuated. Many of our relatives and friends descended on us in Pyinmana but a great number of them packed their valuables and belongings and left the country by ship from Rangoon.'

*

In spite of everything, Christmas was just two days away and a festive spirit was in the air. There was much excitement in the homes of the Goan community in Rangoon. 'Forty pounds of gorgeous Christmas cake made under the supervision of aunts Winnie and Emily had just been baked at Mrs Cheron's Goan bakery,' remembers Donald Menezes who was living with his grandfather, A.J. D'Cruz.

'Mrs Cheron's Bakery on 50th Street was my grandmother's. My mother Ivy's parents, Domingos (a plague victim) and Euphem were proprietors of Cheron Bakery and Confectionery which they had bought from a Frenchman, and hence the name,' says Isabelle. 'My grandmother supplied bread to East Rangoon Goans and on the 23rd she was busy making special plum cakes and roasting stuffed ducks which she supplied annually at Christmas to all who placed their orders with her.'

Lena Rego recalls that December morning in detail. 'We were busy at home preparing little things and getting ready for the big day. In those days there were no readymade stars or decorations and we had to make them at home. On the morning of December 23rd, my sister and I were cutting kite paper and making chains for decorations; one of my brothers was cutting bamboo to make the star, while another brother was practicing "Silent Night, Holy Night" on his violin. The others were doing the usual housework except for one brother, Patrick, who had gone to the dhobi to fetch the curtains and cushion covers we had given for washing and ironing. My parents too had gone shopping for foodstuffs to prepare Christmas sweets.'

Geraldine's father owned the famous Burma Café. Perhaps it was fitting that her mother was busy making the sweet dodol for Christmas with the help of the servant and so Geraldine had to take her younger sister, Julie, to church for her first confession, as she was due to receive her First Holy Communion on Christmas Day.

Wilma Silgardo remembers that her mother was sewing curtains on 23rd December. 'I was at home, as the schools had closed down after the bombing of Pearl Harbour and my school had been turned into a hospital. There were reconnaissance planes that had flown over Rangoon. Many men were given training in ARP (Air-raid Protection), but the actual bombing took place without warning.'

Chapter 3

10.10 am

Even though many of them were young, the survivors all hark back to the surprise bombing of Rangoon by Japanese planes. Donald Menezes' account reveals the shock and terror that they all experienced.

'It was about 10 a.m. on 23 December, 1941, when the Japanese made their first and most devastating attack on Rangoon. Flying in broad daylight at less than 2,000 feet, some twenty-three Japanese planes poured death and destruction upon an unarmed and helpless city. The air-raid sirens had wailed about half-an-hour earlier, but nothing had happened then. So after the initial panic, people relaxed and began moving in the streets, as in the usual practice alerts. After all, 10 a.m. is office hour.

'Then, terror struck!

'First the vroom-vroom-vroom of de-synchronized aircraft engines, then the howl and scream of diving planes. This was followed by the crump and explosion of light bombs and murderous chatter of machine guns. We had seen and heard all this in films and on the radio. But this was for real! And we were the targets. You cannot imagine the terror!

'We could hear our faithful Yeriah running about closing

doors and windows. There must have been thirty doors and windows in all to the house. I ran up to the house again, yelling in Hindustani, "Yeriah, you fool, come down! Leave the windows. All coolies come down! Come down!" Then, halfway up on the landing, my courage failed. The sounds of exploding bombs, the rattling of machine guns, the sirens and the shouts of panic turned my feet back to the trenches. As I ran towards the trenches, I looked up at the sky. Just beyond the overhang of the upper verandah, I saw four black puffs of smoke in the sky in a neat "box". Inside the "box", I saw a Japanese plane disintegrate in the smoke. Our Anglo-Indian ack-ack gunners of the Burma Auxiliary Force had brought down their first Japanese plane. Great guys! I felt a thrill of exhilaration.

'The sound of planes and bomb explosions drew closer and closer, then passed almost overhead. We crouched in terror, praying wordlessly, our heads virtually touching the ground. Suddenly cries broke out: "The street is on fire. Run! Run!" Next moment a terrified human horde bore down the street in dumb panic. Some flooded into our compound, seeking the cover of our mango tree. We could hear their bare feet pattering on the planks and sandbags over our trenches. They were the Chittagonian river-men who lived on 52nd Street nearer the water front. They had been viciously bombed and machine-gunned. Then the horde fled and disappeared up the street.'

Donald's grandfather A.J. D'Cruz recorded in his diary that the exact time was ten minutes past ten in the morning when the bombing began. He tells how they jumped into trenches and later drove to Pazundaung Police Station where there were a couple of hundred evacuees hoping for protection.

Sylvia D'Gama (née Saldanha), another survivor, explains why the bombing came as a surprise although rumours of an imminent Japanese attack were rife: 'On December 23, 1941 the look-out at Monkey Point (the naval point at the tip of Rangoon) mistook the Japanese planes for Allied planes and gave the alert only after the bombs fell. So people were taken by surprise. Before the air-raid sirens sounded, people came out to watch the planes thinking that it was dog-fight practice. Many of those people died on the roadside and soon there was a stench of decaying bodies.'

Lena Rego's parents had gone shopping for foodstuffs to prepare Christmas sweets. They were returning home with a coolie carrying the load of provisions they had bought and were near their house when they heard the sound of planes and machine-guns and bombs falling. They saw the bridge they had just crossed collapse behind them. Fires had started breaking out here and there. 'They desperately started calling out to us children in the building, but we did not hear them because of the violin playing or maybe we were in our own world,' Lena remembers. 'Suddenly one of us heard some screaming and confusion on the street outside. So we ran out to the verandah to see what was happening. Oh! What a dreadful sight! We saw flames everywhere and people all running in one direction,' she exclaims.

Eleven-year-old Albert deSouza's family, consisting of his parents, Anthony Xavier and Mary deSouza, and their four children, was also caught unawares. Albert recalls, 'Around 10 a.m., the sirens sounded but we did not go to the shelter, thinking it was a false alarm. The first explosion was about twenty minutes later and then all hell broke loose. I still remember a gharry tearing down the street, the horse neighing in terror. The din of bombs falling, aircraft flying low and the noise of anti-aircraft guns was frightening. I took refuge under a bed hoping it would offer some degree of protection unless there was a direct hit on the building. At one stage, we ran out of the house in panic but were directed indoors again, since it was safer there. There was the fear of machine-gunning since Japanese pilots would sometimes swoop down low and mow down civilians,' he recalls.

Some of the survivors observed that many of the men in Rangoon had been trained in ARP and they guided people to trenches and basements to take shelter there. Geraldine Pinto of the Burma Café remembers that the Japanese planes 'just dived down Fraser Street and machine-gunned the public. My sister Julie and I and others in the church, including the priests and Bishop, all came out to see what was going on and saw an oil field burning in the distance. We ran into the open trenches and remained there until the all-clear was sounded.'

Eric Menezes, whose father had moved the family out of Rangoon to a nearby suburb, gives a vivid description of what he witnessed from a distance: 'About ninety Japanese aircraft, bombers and escorting fighters flew in from the south west. It became clear that these formations headed towards Rangoon in waves. Anti-aircraft fire began almost immediately. Hundreds of black puffs of exploding shells filled the sky and I personally saw three Japanese planes explode in the sky and the fourth, trailing smoke, go a little further before blowing up. We were told later that in this air-raid the Japanese lost nine planes.'

*

Records state that on the morning of 23 December, 1941, fifty-four jet bombers escorted by twenty-four fighter planes attacked Rangoon. It was estimated that about 2,500 people were killed and many more injured.

Chapter 4

Horror, Death and Destruction

'We came out of our trench as the marshals ran down the streets, blowing their whistles and ordering evacuation,' recalls Donald Menezes. 'As we went upstairs to salvage important personal belongings and documents, my grandfather wept. Would his beautiful house and life savings go up in smoke?

'Soon the streets were empty, with inhabitants directed to the neighbouring Thingangyut Police Station. Then, Arnold, my youngest uncle (younger than me!) and I went up the street to see about the fires. The Sailors' Homes, a shelter for white foreign seamen, had been hit and had burned to the ground. But miraculously, no one had been killed. Some seamen were sitting in the upstairs balcony when the bomb hit. The house collapsed like a pack of cards, and as the balcony hit the ground, the men leapt out and ran for their lives. Others escaped by leaping out of doors and windows. In ten minutes flat, the house was reduced to ashes. The phosphorus pellets emitted from the bombs had ignited fires. Two trees in the compound were ablaze, and the fire had spread to the roof of the adjacent house. Just then, a fire engine arrived and the hose was run out and brought into action. Arnold and I gave them a helping hand. With crowbar and axe, the firemen broke into the locked upstairs of the burning house. Suddenly Arnold and I found ourselves alone with the hose. It twisted like a demon in our hands and broke loose, falling to the ground. Arnold flung himself in a rugby tackle on the hose, and I followed suit. We got it up and into action. At that moment, a fireman opened a window of the burning house and the water blast hit him in the face. There was a laugh from the few bystanders who had collected. With the fires out, Arnold and I ran off to the recreation centre to tell our family the good news. Everyone was happy.

'Suddenly we heard a high-pitched cry, "Mr D'Cruz! Mr D'Cruz! Winnie! Emily! Eddie is dead! Eddie is dead!" The tragic news about my Uncle Eddie was brought by Ronnie D'Souza, who lived on the next street, close to Eddie's house. Grandpa and the aunts broke out crying and moaning as Ronnie cried out the news. We all loved Eddie so much. Arnold and I jumped into Uncle Eddie's car which Ronnie had come in, along with the Pathan driver, and sped to Eddie's house. The bomb had torn a hole in the lower half of the iron grill-work of his front porch. Through this hole, Eddie had crawled on elbows and arms and called on a passer-by to save his family. He was carried to a passing ambulance and Ronnie saw him and spoke to him before he died.

'As Arnold and I entered Uncle's house, we were met by a scene of horror and death. Aunt Connie's body had fallen forward from the piano stool in a semi-upright position. Her head, bashed in by the bomb blast, rested face down on the radio set. She had delivered her baby, due that day. It lay dead on the floor. Blood, bones, brains and limbs lay scattered around. But there were no recognisable bodies. However, three others had died in that bomb blast; a five-year-old child, Winsome, her Burmese nanny, and Connie's mother, Mrs Marshner.

'As we sped along the roads to the Rangoon General Hospital where Uncle Eddie had been taken, we saw corpses by the dozens, lying on the roads. Machine-gun bullets had cut open heads and stomachs, spilling out brains and guts. Great holes were gouged in the roads, with water spewing out of burst water mains. Buildings were still burning. Some leaned drunkenly, as if about to collapse. No one really knew the death toll. The estimates were between 3,000 and 10,000 killed and wounded. Mr Scully, a tenant of my grandfather and a dock engineer, told us the dead were in the thousands at the docks. It was a bloody massacre.

'At the hospital, we saw the body of Uncle Eddie. His face was handsome, smiling peacefully in death, as he had smiled in life. That was the last we ever saw of Uncle Eddie and his family. We know not how or where their bodies were buried or burnt—probably in mass graves or cremations.

'Thousands of bodies were unidentified. The city of Rangoon emptied in a few hours. Forty-eight hours later, a mass of fleeing Indians were reported at Prome, nearly two hundred miles north of Rangoon, as they fled by bus, truck, train, bullock-cart, push-cart and bicycle and on foot, anything that moved, carrying their few personal belongings.'

A.J. D'Cruz explains why his son Eddie's house was targeted: 'My son was living on Thompson Street and parked all around his house were the motor trucks which used to ply between Rangoon and China, carrying all materials including arms for the use of the Chinese forces. The Japanese planes spotted the trucks from the air and became furious, like bulls spotting a red rag. They bombed the trucks indiscriminately, turning them into something like matchboxes. Unfortunately, however, one of the bombs fell on the upper storey of the house in which my son was living. It passed through the roof, upper-storey flooring, and burst on the ground floor in the midst of the family, killing all six members of my son's family.'

Thelma Menezes, who urged me to write this book, and her brother were resident students of Judson College in Rangoon at that time while their father, Lal Mohan Ghosh, a lawyer who had come from Calcutta, and her mother, Margery, an Anglo-Burmese lady, lived in Pegu 45 miles away from Rangoon. She recalls the scramble to get out of Rangoon. 'Trying to escape from the city, we got caught up in frenzied crowds laden with luggage, desperately scrambling for seats in trains and buses. Air-raid sirens screamed overhead and the air was foul with putrefying corpses. We managed to reach Pegu and as the air-raids continued, my family evacuated to Myingyan where my mother's relatives lived.'

Thelma observed that when Japan began the invasion of Burma with the aerial bombardment of Rangoon, it was reported that for the first time in history basic conventions had been flouted. Residential areas became strategic targets. Thousands of innocent civilians who happened to be on the streets or out in the open were systematically gunned down by low-flying planes. Bullets ripped open heads and stomachs. 'It was a killing field,' she said with a sigh.

Lena Rego says, 'We quickly rushed down the steps to our parents, and the whole family except my brother Patrick—who had not yet returned from the dhobi—ran to the nearby St. Mary's Cathedral and took shelter underground, where the bishops were buried. What we saw on the way was horrible! The hawkers by the roadside with their heads knocked off, the hands, legs and body parts of so many others, scattered about, and those who were not dead, screaming and crying out loud in fear and confusion.'

'The bombardment of Rangoon was intense and terrible,' says Eric Menezes. 'We were told of inexperienced people who were standing in the street and watching the planes, being machine-gunned or blown to bits along with buildings. Whole lines of shops in the Surtee Bazaar were strafed by Japanese fighters, leaving hundreds dead. The raid lasted for a little over half an hour; towards the end of this, Daddy raced in from the city, literally turning into our gate on two wheels. The first thing he did was to rush us into the air-raid shelter which he had dug a few days earlier. It may seem stupid, but during the raid we were all standing in the garden, mesmerised, stomachs churning, frozen with fright, watching Rangoon burn in the distance and feeling the shock waves of bursting bombs. During this first time at least, we could not tear our eyes away from the battle and the destruction taking place.'

Albert deSouza remembers that the ground shook and reverberated. 'Ten miles away from our suburb of Gyogon was Rangoon Port, which was burning from the intense bombing. After the raid, we could see dense black clouds rising into the sky, probably caused by incendiary bombs dropped on the docks.'

Geraldine Pinto adds: 'A cousin of mine unfortunately ran towards the planes, thinking they were coming from the opposite direction and was killed. Another escaped with a bullet just grazing past his shoe. The British chased the Japanese and so they just dropped their bombs as they fled. One dropped near Burma Café. My brother, Joseph, who was helping in the café lay flat on the ground and managed to avoid the machine-gun fire and splinters or else he would have been killed. The bullets knocked down a big tin of jam that was on the shelf and my father was saved by the door of the safe which he had opened to remove some money. Else he would have been injured.'

Sylvia D'Gama also has memories of that fateful day. 'I was on the second floor of the building when I heard the frightening sounds. My brother Len ran out to see what was happening. There was a fire burning nearby in Eddie D'Cruz's house and he found that a direct hit had killed almost the entire family. My eldest brother came home from the office but my elder sister, who was a nurse, stayed on at the hospital to attend to her patients. All the nurses and other staff went to take shelter in the open trenches, but my sister refused to leave the frightened patients. The irony of it was that some of the people in the trenches died, when the burning wing of a plane fell on them, while those in the hospital survived. My mother too refused to go down into the trench below our building, because she wanted to finish the Christmas pudding that she was in the process of making.'

Wilma Silgardo heard the sounds of planes zooming in the sky and bombs exploding. 'When I looked out of the window I saw a plane disintegrate and the burning pieces falling on the road. Later, three bodies were found on the steps of our music shop,' she remembers.

*

This was the first wave of bombing in Rangoon. In the days that followed, sirens wailed at odd hours, alerting the people to run into trenches and hide till the all-clear sounded. New trenches were dug. All lamps were fitted with black conical shades, which directed electric light only onto the floor. Glass window panes were pasted with strips of brown paper, besides being covered with heavy drapes. Cotton ear plugs and wooden pencils to clamp teeth were provided to prevent children from hearing or making too much noise.

Life in the city was paralysed. About 100,000 people, mostly Indian workmen, stayed away from the dockyards and the Burma Railway. Thousands of them began a mass exodus from Rangoon. Indians feared that with the breakdown of law and order, a Burmese mob would loot and attack them. The Burmans, unlike the other ethnic minorities such as the Shans, Karens, Kachins or Chins, harboured racial animosity against the Indians in Burma, especially after the anti-Indian riots of May 1930 that followed a strike of Indian coolies at the Rangooon Harbour. (The British colonial authorities noted that 120 Indians were killed and 900 were injured in the riots. Recent investigations have suggested that they had under-reported the violence: about 200 died and 2,000 were injured.) Besides, the Burmese were on the Japanese side now, while the Indians lived under the protective umbrella of the British. Insecure and panic stricken, they fled the Japanese invasion on foot, heading towards India.

Chapter 5

Thereafter: 24 December 1941 to April 1942

At the time, Britain was engaged in the Second World War and the bulk of the Indian Army was deployed across the world to keep the Germans and Italians at bay. The British were unprepared for the invasion of Burma and were inadequately equipped to counter the onslaught. The Japanese launched several air-raids on Rangoon and nearby Mingaladon airport over the next five months. Unable to bring troops, planes or tanks from far-off Europe and the Middle East in time to stop the Japanese forces, they were forced to retreat to Upper Burma. The Japanese invasion was swift and well-planned. Besides the air-raids, Japanese troops, together with the Burma Independence Army, entered Burma through Thailand. Rangoon fell on March 8, 1942. There was chaos in the city. Inmates of mental asylums, lepers and convicts were let loose, wandering the city, looting and adding to the prevailing confusion. Animals in the zoo were shot dead or set free because there was no one to take care of them.

By May 1942, the Japanese greatly outnumbered the British army men. They were seasoned fighters who had overrun Hong Kong, Malaya (now Malaysia), Thailand and had come to Burma well trained in jungle warfare. They also possessed superior weapons and equipment. Advancing with speed and great force, they pushed the troops of the British and the Allied Indian Army, who suffered heavy losses, through Northern Burma, back to the Indian borders.

The Goans of Rangoon had to make crucial decisions. For many, their first plan of action was to move out of their homes in the heart of Rangoon where the bombing was the heaviest. Word was passed around that since it was comparatively safer in the suburbs, they should move to the bungalows where their Goan friends were living.

*

Anju D'Souza, Isabelle's father, moved his family out of Rangoon to the Menezes residence in the suburb of Kokine. A few other Goan families did the same. Eric Menezes remembered that many had made fun of his father for taking this precaution of renting the bungalow in Kokine and moving there a few weeks before the bombing. 'But,' he continues, 'we of course welcomed them, as it was good to have your own people around you. The Silgardos came in a few days later. The spare bedrooms were allocated and all was cosy with a sense of safety that comes with numbers.

'On Christmas Eve, Daddy, Mummy and one of the Mandrick brothers, with me in tow, went into Rangoon ostensibly to see if our two houses were safe. One of them was; but bright, cheerful Rangoon was no more. We had to make several detours around destroyed buildings and the dead and the debris were still being cleared. The city was mournful and overcast with hazy smoke. Very few people were on the streets, apart from occasional armed police patrols and ARP men and what was unnerving in the general silence was the mournful howling of dogs. Looters had not yet put in an appearance, but none of us wished to remain in town. After collecting our Christmas cake which had been previously ordered and taking a few things Mummy required from the house, we returned to Kokine.

'The next day, December 25th, we got our Christmas present in the shape of another heavy bombardment by the Japanese. This time, we reacted with experience and all took shelter in the trenches where we could hear the sound of continuous explosions and feel the ground tremble under our feet. Curiosity was too strong, however and, from time to time, one or two of the elders would climb out of the trench and report on the battles raging in the air, of planes being shot down, and of course Rangoon burning and covered by clouds of smoke. This time, British aircraft, assisted by some American planes from the "Chennault raiders"—under the leadership of Lieutenant General Claire-Lee Chennault who wielded together a bunch of mercenaries and adventurers to form a crack flying unit—did put in an appearance towards the end of the raid, and both sides lost some planes in the dog fights.

'The Japanese, however, achieved their objective. The terror they created began a mass exodus from Rangoon. Everybody, especially the Indians, wanted to get out. All roads going to the north of Burma were soon choked with refugees all wanting to get to India, many hundreds of miles away. No arrangements had been made for such traffic and thus began the "Great Trek" in which nobody knows how many thousands died.

'On the evening of December 25th, our two South Indian

servants announced that they were leaving for home along with a group of their compatriots. There was nothing else to do but to give them some rice, sugar, a little oil and two hundred rupees to meet expenses on the way. In the nervousness and excitement, our cooks had forgotten to prepare lunch and time was spent talking fearfully of what might happen next. We never saw them again. The ayah stayed on but I do not know what she did after we left.

'The events of the day were not yet over. Our landlords, the Gardners, themselves decided to leave and offered to sell the entire bungalow to Daddy for the throwaway price of only five thousand rupees, which Dad had to decline as we did not know our own future. Apart from a few slices, the Christmas cake was uneaten and nobody had any inclination to enjoy the small Christmas lunch.

'Horror stories of what had happened in Rangoon proper continued to pour in: of buildings being blown to bits, huge number of civilians killed and wounded, and also of how the Japanese pilots machine-gunned to death hundreds of people who did not understand the barbaric nature of the enemy and did not know how to protect themselves. We at Kokine Lakes were spared all this, but we could see the formations of enemy aircraft overhead on their way to Rangoon, hear the deafening roar of over a hundred engines, the thunder of anti-aircraft guns, anti-aircraft shells exploding in the sky, or an occasional aircraft hit and brought down in flames, which gave us much joy. There also was the sight of Japanese planes making passes over their targets in Rangoon, planes screaming down in dives, hearing the terrible sound of exploding bombs and the ground trembling with the shockwaves. Above all was the strange and morbid fascination to watch this destruction, the burning and the dense pall of smoke which covered the Rangoon city skyline.

'We were all terribly afraid. I remember Mummy praying the rosary whilst sheltering in the trenches and me clutching my air-gun as if it was a means of defence. It is curious that at this stage I developed a minor ailment which finally disappeared after almost a decade. Otherwise, Kokine was quite safe, despite the fact that it was close to the Mingaladon airport. Perhaps the Japanese wanted it for their own use later and it was also a fact that there was nothing much to bomb there anyway. So the next two days, December 26th and 27th were days of rest, so to say.

'The Gardners left on December 27th; their two servants also disappeared. Mr Gardner requested Daddy to look after the house and to please stay there as long as we could or liked. The next day, the Burmese watchman told Daddy that he too would be leaving. So, regretfully, Daddy gave him ten George V silver rupees, and he too left. He did not have to do anything much, but it was nice to have a local man around, especially at night, and he was armed.

'The household now comprised ourselves and our Goan friends (refugees who moved in for shelter on December 25th), in all about eighteen people, including us four children and five not too very brave men, since the servants were all gone. The ladies took over the household work, including cooking meals. Since there was still no shortage of fresh vegetables and other foodstuffs, things were okay.

'On December 29th, Daddy took us to town. Rangoon was now a dismal place, with heavy bomb damage, vestiges of smoke, very few people on the streets and, those few moving quickly. There was silence. Even in the daytime, gloom had descended on the city together with a peculiar smell of smoke and rot. There were lots of dogs moving about, and what worried Daddy the most was the possibility of looters. There were a few patrols of police and soldiers with rifles. A convoy of British troops in buses, all singing lustily and making a great deal of noise, passed us on our return to Kokine. They were going to the front, down south beyond Moulmein and were a heartening sight; but Mummy felt sorry for them as the war news was not at all good, with the Japanese giving the Allies a beating almost everywhere. We collected a few things from the Rangoon house, which was intact.

'In all, I remember eight bombardments from the air by the Japanese between December 23, 1941 and January 26, 1942 but I cannot give the dates, especially of those in January. We had a good plastering on December 31st to close the year. On this occasion we saw some Japanese pilots parachute from their planes which were hit. The story went around that as these parachutists floated towards the ground, lots of people ran to see them or perhaps even capture them, but the Japanese opened fire, killing several of these people. This had an interesting sequel which may seem extremely funny now but was certainly not a joke at that time. During one of the subsequent bombings, when we were all cowering inside the trenches or bomb shelter, one of our ladies peeped outside the entrance and looked upwards and started screaming "parachutist". Almost at once everyone was screaming in panic. Fortunately it turned out to be a large eagle's feather, brown and white, which had come loose and was floating earthwards. This woman's imagination did the rest, but one can understand the fear and the tension.

'Fireworks on December 31st, New Year's Eve morning, had been provided by the Japanese and bringing in the New Year was a lifeless affair. The usual midnight salutations were forgotten and by now, we children had learned to play within the dim circles of light on the floor which was all the black conical lamp shades would allow. Come evening, the heavy curtains were always drawn.

'January 1, 1942 was a nice day and although there was no Christmas tree at Christmas time, I had already got my presents earlier and we all played with my train set, the soldiers and the Meccano Set No 3. We also played in the garden and had a pleasant time. New Year's lunch was also good with Mummy's stuffed roast chicken, sliced ham, the usual rice and curry and, of course, cake left over from Christmas; there was lots of it still left. The elders (men) were all drinking in the hall and no doubt discussing the situation but we children played on until called for lunch. As I said before, we were relatively unaffected by what had happened just the day before in Rangoon and earlier. Perhaps one quickly learned to make the best of the situations even in bad circumstances. Speaking about Japanese air attacks, the people always seemed to know when they would come and many people observed that there was a well-organised spy system by the Japanese in Burma. Nevertheless, the wailing of sirens always brought about a turning of one's stomach and one can only imagine the feelings of those in the actual danger zones. No bombs fell in our immediate vicinity and in this we were extremely fortunate.

'The actual brush that I had with a Japanese plane was some time during the first week of January 1942. The ayah, carrying my brother Leslie and me, had ventured outside our garden on what was supposed to be a quiet morning. We had crossed the Mingaladon airport road which went past our house and were strolling in the open field along the road. Apparently the Japanese had staged a light air-raid, and when the sirens went off we were still in the open field about two hundred yards away from the road and home. I remember there were three British Beaufighters in the air having a dog-fight with the Japanese and they were flying quite close above our heads, as we hurried home. It seemed as though one enemy plane was trying to dive on us several times only to be headed off by one of the Beaufighters, and thus we escaped being machine-gunned.

'So the days passed. What came in were occasional air raids, bad news of the Japanese army advancing up the Malay Peninsula and the increasing realisation that the British would not be able to hold them off, despite the trickle of reinforcement British and Indian troops from India. Worse still, the schools were closed and I had not attended any classes since the first week of December. I had just started learning the piano but this instrument was in Rangoon in the town house.

'Gloomy faces, a gloomy atmosphere and a definite drop in morale was obvious and we experienced the necessity of living from one day to the next. Although we had no shortage of food, there was no doubt that it was a hopeless situation. By the middle of January, Daddy must have decided that something would have to be done to get us out.

At this point in time, the Japanese navy was more or less supreme in the Pacific Ocean bordering all the landmasses in Southeast Asia and that portion of the Indian Ocean around Java and Sumatra, up to Australia. But, they had not made their presence felt in Indian waters and in particular, the Bay of Bengal. There were reports of some submarine activity but no action by surface vessels nor any systematic interception and sinking of cargo or passenger vessels. As a result, movement by sea was still in operation although normal blackout procedures were followed.

'There were still more or less regular ships sailing from Rangoon to and fro between Indian ports like Calcutta, Visakhapatnam, Madras. It was the best bet for evacuation as the alternative, trekking, was not to be thought of and almost certainly a death warrant.

'The second and third week of January ran their drab course, and there were three or four additional air attacks although not of their initial ferocity. But the situation was definitely turning worse and we were advised to get out before it became too late.'

*

Isabelle Vaz, who was one of the children taking refuge in the Menezes' Kokine house, remembers the fun amidst the fear. 'We children had fun in the open spaces; but as soon as we heard or spotted a plane we would all dive into the trenches. We stayed there till we were told it was okay to come out. New trenches were dug, and we spent many days and nights in these. The men motored to and fro from Kokine to central Rangoon by day. The ladies, who were so used to cooks and servants, had to do their own cooking. Often rice turned pish-pash on coal fires, when cooking had to be abandoned till the all-clear sirens sounded. All of us went for Mass, Confession and Holy Communion at the nearby church, so as to be prepared for death. We survived, but grieved for those who didn't.'

*

The Sequeira family, considered to be the richest Goan family in Burma, had a country residence on Ady Road near the Kokine Lakes, which, for some reason, wasn't targeted by the Japanese bomber planes. 'Word was passed around that East Rangoon Goans should proceed there for their safety. By sunset, around 6 p.m., the last batch of us had arrived there, bringing all the provisions we had stored for Christmas, including Christmas cake, duck, chicken and all the Christmas sweets,' says Donald Menezes. 'Those minutes of the bombing of Rangoon by the Japanese had changed all our lives irrevocably,' he adds. 'For ten days, we stayed at Kokine Lakes, bathing and swimming in the lake, singing, dancing, dallying with the girls, playing with the kids, joking with the elders and dashing for the trenches when the sirens sounded. Our cheerfulness and helpfulness buoyed up the elderly. The subject of Uncle Eddie and the D'Cruz tragedy was taboo, because it had a terrible effect on Grandpa and Aunt Emily. Those who came to condole were told to quickly change the subject.

'The remarkable thing in this whole episode was the general high spirits. In that group of about ten families, everyone recalls this period as a great "fun time". The only occupations were cooking, eating, sleeping and fooling around between raids. We gorged ourselves on Christmas cake, sorpotel, pulao, duck and all the goodies prepared by the families for Christmas.

'Air-raid warnings came at all hours, but mostly at dusk when the Japanese sent in planes in ones or twos to immobilise the Mingaladon airport. Night raids were more frightening, because old people and children had to be moved in the dark, after being awakened from their sleep. Moonlight outside the house, however, helped.

'Once in broad daylight on New Year's Day, we saw three flights of Japanese planes pass directly overhead at less than 1,000 feet. From our trenches concealed in a grove of tall trees, we saw distinctly their markings—the Rising Sun of Japan. Then, in the distance, we could see them bombing Rangoon Harbour. Great billows of smoke rose in the sky. But we were safe, thank God!

'We could not stay indefinitely at Kokine. The Japanese ground forces had already crossed Thailand and captured Moulmein (currently Mawlamyaing, on the Tenasserim coast in south-east Burma). On January 4th, our advance party proceeded to the Rangoon Railway Station and took the train to Mandalay and then across the beautiful Ava Bridge to Monywa on the Lower Chindwin River. From there we proceeded to Mawlaik on a paddle steamer of the Irrawadi Flottilla Co. Mawlaik had no access by rail or by road.

'My grandfather was so badly affected by the tragedy of Uncle Eddie and his family that he was in constant distress and could not sleep. I was his emotional and physical support. No one else could cope with him. So by six in the morning, after hot tea and toast, I walked with him on the streets of Mawlaik which was covered by a dense fog in winter up to 10 a.m. Grandfather would stop everyone who could speak a little English or Hindustani and tell them of his family tragedy. Soon he was the object of compassion for the officials, tradesmen, clerks, hospital ward boys and chowkidars.'

Donald Menezes also comments on what he calls Japan's strategic mastery of the air. 'There were two reasons why the Japanese did not carry out constant air attacks. They only mounted nuisance raids. Their major raids had been costly in terms of planes and pilots and were now unnecessary. Secondly, they had achieved complete strategic mastery in the first attack on Rangoon, which had paralyzed the city. No more did supplies flow to Chiang Kai Shek's armies in central and western China. Rangoon was defended by a squadron of obsolete Brewster Buffaloes. They were no match for Japanese planes. The Royal Air Force (RAF) squadron is reported to have refused to send up their men to certain death. But the American Flying Tigers, fighting under the command of Lieutenant-General Claire-Lee Chennault in Chungking, dispatched a squadron to defend Rangoon. They had barely set up, when the first Japanese raid came in. The American Tomahawks pursued the Japanese like avenging demons right up to the Thailand border, reportedly shooting down twenty-one out of twenty-three raiding planes. A similar slaughter was alleged on the New Year's Day Japanese raid.'

*

Donald's grandfather, A.J. D'Cruz, recounts, 'Eventually, at the request of my son Victor, we all migrated to Mawlaik on January 7, 1942, leaving behind Arnold and Robert, who had to recover all valuable papers and jewellery which were deposited in the strong room of the Mercantile Bank, along with the valuables of A. Fraser Ltd. I also left the car which was to be used by them in case the Railway services were interrupted. We arrived at Monywa the following day and the Civil Surgeon of the place, Dr Crane, met us at the station, at Victor's request. He took us to his house and made us comfortable till 10.30 p.m. when he accompanied us to the ferry boat that plied between Monywa and Mawlaik. We arrived at Mawlaik on the third day after leaving Monywa, and Victor came on the boat and took us to his house where we made our stay for three months, again thinking that the Japanese would go away.

'Arnold and Robert tried to get out the documents which had been deposited in the Chartered Bank strong room, along with those belonging to A. Fraser Ltd. But the bombing in Rangoon was continuous and they took a month to secure the documents with the help of my son's assistant, H. Kelly. After Arnold secured the documents, the next job was to get away from Rangoon. Robert had gone off to Akyab where his parents were and Arnold, who was left alone, had to frighten off the goondas who used to attack the house daily. By this time, the railway station was wiped out of existence and the train service between Rangoon and Mandalay had stopped. In spite of these difficulties, he had to find his way to us at Mawlaik. He had the car at his disposal but no petrol could be got anywhere. He went all over in search of petrol, but without success. Finally he went to the port commissioner's warehouse and godown. There he met an old acquaintance who asked him what he wanted. When he was told that Arnold wanted petrol, the godown keeper said, "Help yourself to as much as you want. There is no owner for all this property."

'Arnold filled his tank and loaded thirty tins of two

gallons each, took the cook in the car and left Rangoon for Mawlaik, travelling by day only. He took the road from Rangoon to Prome and then to Magwe, Yenangyaung and Mandalay, crossed the Ava Bridge to Sagaing and arrived at Monywa (more than 400 miles from Rangoon). Here, he had to abandon the car and the remaining tins of petrol because there was no further road beyond Monywa. He then went on the ferry boat towards Mawlaik. The boat was so over-crowded due to the great rush of Indian evacuees and the confusion that prevailed there, that she sailed a small distance and got stuck in the mud. They remained in that position for some days. In the meantime, Arnold spied a motor boat coming towards Monywa. He shouted out to the men and was told that it belonged to the Deputy Commissioner of Mawlaik. Then he told the serang (skipper) that he was the brother of Dr D'Cruz, the Civil Surgeon, and asked that he be taken on board, to which the serang agreed. To our great surprise, they arrived at Mawlaik the following day, while we were having lunch. As the whole family and my grandchildren, Donald and Muriel, were together, we remained at Mawlaik for three months.

'While at Mawlaik, I was much worried and unhappy for obvious reasons. When in Rangoon I was in the habit of visiting the church every evening, but when I arrived at Mawlaik I found there was no church nor was there any hope of meeting any priest in those parts. We wrote to the Bishop of Mandalay, but he said he found difficulty in carrying on the church services even at his headquarters at Mandalay for want of priests. The thought that there was no church or any priest to console me in my affliction worried me. The loss I had sustained from the death of my son and his family, and also the loss of my house and all it contained, touched my heart very deeply. I had disposed of my ancestral property in India and with the proceeds from the sale, invested in this house in Rangoon. I had planned to spend the remainder of my life in this sanctified home I had built myself. I had carried away nothing from my house at the time of my evacuation.

'While at Mawlaik, I used to meet all the Goan and Anglo-Indian evacuees passing through. One day, a Goan lady, rather old and ill, arrived along with her daughter and daughter-in-law. They could not proceed further so they took up a room in the bazaar quarter. When I heard of their arrival I went in search of them and found them. The old woman was in a bad state of health. Her name was Mrs D'Souza and she was related to the Cherons of Rangoon. Her son, Daniel, was in the health department and was working under my son Victor at this time. Her son was away, so was my son, attending to the thousands of evacuees who were going to India by the Kalewa–Tamu Road. I asked Dr Reddy, Assistant Surgeon of the hospital, to attend to the old woman. He reported that she would not live for more than three days and charged those people five rupees for his visit. After my son returned, I told him all about the woman. He brought her to the hospital and accommodated the daughter and daughter-in-law in a building vacated by one of the nurses who was on leave.

The old woman died in three days and her body was moved to the nurses' quarters. Now there was no undertaker there to do the needful for the disposal of the body and the two young women could do nothing. So I made enquiries and one Mr Edwards offered to help me. He brought some

Burmese carpenters who made a long box to be used as a coffin. I inquired and found that there was a Christian burial ground at Mawlaik in which several Europeans of the B.B.T.C. Ltd (Bombay Burma Trading Corporation Limited) were buried. I obtained the necessary permission from the Deputy Commissioner's office, paid for the ground and for digging the grave, invited all Christians from the evacuees' camp and carried out the funeral prayers myself according to the Daily Missal and buried the woman. Some thirty evacuees attended the funeral.'

A few months after the first edition of *Songs of the Survivors* was released, a nun from Goa came up to thank me with tears in her eyes because she now knew that her grandmother, this Mrs D'Souza, had been taken care of and had had a proper burial. The family had always assumed that the grandmother died during the trek and her body was left lying unburied by the track and this had saddened them.

A.J. D'Cruz continues his story: 'While at Mawlaik, two weddings took place. In both cases the brides were Catholics. We tried to get a priest from Mandalay but did not succeed, so I gave the Deputy Commissioner my Daily Missal and he carried on the services as laid down therein. One wedding took place on Good Friday. This could not be helped as the bridegroom was going away to join his post early the following morning. The reception of one wedding was held in the Circuit House and that of the other in the Mawlaik Club. For both weddings, all local officials and their families were invited. We managed to get a piano and violin and I played several dance pieces and all the guests danced and enjoyed themselves. Refreshments were plentiful and everybody had a good time.'

*

Sylvia D'Gama remembers that practically every night, there was bombing in Rangoon and they had to run into the trenches whenever the sirens sounded. 'We had been trained to feel for our coats, solar topees and shoes in the dark before running out. It was fun for us kids and we used to have fun in the trenches too. At first, the trenches were uncovered but later planks and zinc sheets or sacks were placed over them. By mid-January 1942, my mother and three of us children were told to go to Mandalay (400 miles from Rangoon) as it was safer there. But immediately after we reached there, we were told to come back to Rangoon and leave by ship for India.'

*

Thelma Menezes recalls the panic that was apparent everywhere. 'All around people fled, carrying what they could, abandoning the rest. All the while, British propaganda gave false hopes and assurances on the radio.' Thelma also gives one a pleasant surprise by relating how she became a bride in the middle of the war. She was just sixteen years old and in love with her Mathematics teacher, Caesar Menezes. 'On February 14, 1942, Caesar and I got married in Myingyan in a quiet ceremony blessed by Fr. Henry. Then we left for Monywa where my in-laws and friends were living together in a rented house.'

She narrates some events that happened to other Goan families. 'There was Charles Macellin, also known as Maxy Machado from Saligao, his wife Matilda Marie (née de San

Lazaro) from Margao, and their three young children. Maxy, a station-master on duty at Pyinmana, was suffering from shellshock. He had swallowed mustard gas dropped by the enemy, burning him inside, making him scream for water. When the roof of the station caved in, his four dogs lying on his back saved his life, but it left him traumatised.

'His wife Matilda came from a musical family, and, before her marriage, used to accompany her brother James on the piano, providing music for silent films in Rangoon. Her sister-in-law, Jessie San Lazaro, James's widow, had also fled from Rangoon with six children, leaving behind a well-established music business. We were all uprooted, uncertain of the future, making collective decisions. We would all meet in Belgaum in India since Maxy wanted a quiet place.'

*

Lena Rego continues her story. 'When the bombing stopped, we went back home, but every day we had to run to the shelter under the cathedral or to other trenches when the siren was given and come out only when the all-clear siren sounded. Food had to be eaten at any time while we were in the house. Sometimes we were given free food like rice, dal, potatoes boiled together and that is how we survived. But it was terrible seeing people dying every day and others suffering, wounded or abandoned, as everyone had to look out for themselves. Life went on like this for weeks.'

*

Felicity Fernandes—of the brother named Crescent and the dog named Nero—lived in Kalaw, which is about 266 miles from Rangoon and they did not directly experience the bombing till March and April 1942. 'When the war finally touched Kalaw, our lives changed drastically. We remember that we had to cover all our windows with black cloth so that no light would be seen from outside and, if it did, there would be a loud knock on the door from the police patrolling the area. The streets were deserted by 6 p.m. as everyone had to be indoors. There were no more outings, no more visits to the parks and no school as well. Dad thought the war would be over in no time and had made no arrangements for leaving Kalaw, just like a great many other people. But it soon became clear that we had to go back to India.'

*

Tony Machado's family too came to the same conclusion. 'Despite the British propaganda, it became clear to us that, contrary to what they said, the Japanese could not be resisted and we decided to flee the country. It was a collective decision because there were more than forty people boarding and lodging with us. My father had to stay behind because he held an important position in the Railways and was also Chief of Civil Defence. More importantly, he was on the verge of retirement after twenty-two years of service so the stakes were high and it would be deemed abandonment of service to leave. So he commissioned a bogie and despatched us to Monywa, the northern terminus of the railway.

'The Japanese advance was swift. The British were caught napping. Mingaladon airport near Rangoon was captured with some RAF planes sitting intact. The British planes manned by Japanese flew down to Pyinmana and bombed the place. Dad was injured and in a state of shock. We were still in Monywa, so as soon as we heard the news a cousin went back and rescued him. It must have been an anxious time for Mum, but the family was soon reunited with Dad and we started up the Chindwin River.'

Chapter 6

We Have to Flee

During the Japanese invasion nearly 400,000 refugees, most of whom were Indians, Anglo-Indians or Anglo-Burmese, became a responsibility and great problem for the British. Before Rangoon fell, about 70,000 Indians had left Burma by sea or by plane. When these exit routes were blocked, the only option left for thousands more was to set out on foot, hundreds of miles to the Indo-Burmese borders with the Japanese on their heels. From January to March 1942, the British government made arrangements to evacuate women and children by ship to Calcutta and Madras. The ships had to dodge torpedoes from Japanese submarines and avoid bomber planes in the Bay of Bengal, so the journey took eight to ten days.

*

Sylvia D'Gama left Rangoon for Calcutta with her family. 'My mother and five of us children boarded the last ship that had been arranged to evacuate people to India,' she says. 'If I recall correctly, there must have been more than three thousand passengers on a ship meant to carry not more than half that number. The toilets were overflowing. It was so cramped and crowded that we had to take turns to lie down. Two of us sat upright while two of us slept. What was supposed to have been a three-day journey took seven days. Instead of crossing the Bay of Bengal, the ship went along the coast to avoid the bomber planes and torpedoes. On the fourth day we ran out of food and I remember eating rusks and nothing else for the remainder of the journey. But thankfully we landed in Calcutta safely and were given food and shelter there.'

*

Doris D'Mello (née D'Souza), whom I interviewed a few months before she passed away from cancer, also shared some of her story of travelling out to India by ship with her family. Her grandfather, Anthony Francis D'Souza, had first gone to Burma and started a grocery store in Thaton, Lower Burma, and later, his three sons, one of whom was Doris' father, followed in his footsteps and opened their own stores. They were so well known as to have a road—D'Souza Street—named after them in Thaton. 'We were told to evacuate to India and fortunately we managed to get seats on the last ship that carried refugees to India. The Portuguese captain (we were told later) didn't know the way as he had to take a roundabout route to avoid the torpedoes. So the voyage which would normally have taken three or four days took fifteen. The ship was overcrowded and we could not get a cabin so we had to spend all the time on the deck. Toilets were not sufficient for all the people and neither was the food which ran out in a few days. We survived on Marie biscuits for the rest of the journey. But when we landed at Madras we were given clothes, food and money,' she remembers.

*

Lena Rego says that amidst all the confusion, they got news that there were steamers to take people to India. 'The steamer jetty was far from our house, so we had to walk from street to street, entering any house and eating whatever we found there. Lots of people had to survive this way, and I'm sure someone entered our house and helped themselves to the food we had left behind too!

'We slowly came towards the jetty, with only a few necessities and valuables, but we were anxious because my brother Patrick was still not found. My big brother went in search of him and even went to look in a van where corpses and limbs were being thrown in to be taken away. Instead of finding Patrick, he saw a lady still alive calling out to him saying, "I'm not dead, please take me out." Hardly had she uttered these words when more limbs and corpses were thrown over her. My brother could do nothing. Disappointed, he continued his search with a heavy heart. But God came to his help, because just as he turned into the road leading to the jetty he saw Patrick coming towards him and we were once again all united as a family. The only sad thing was that my brother Lucas, who was already eighteen years old, was not allowed on the ship because priority was being given to the children, women and old. Anyway, we prayed that he would find his way to India.

'Even on the ship, we were filled with fear as there was danger of torpedoes in the water and bomber planes overhead killing us on the ocean. We cried together and prayed together, thinking that these were our last moments to live.

On the second day of our voyage, we saw a ship coming towards us. Assuming that it was a Japanese ship, people started screaming and crying; but we thanked God when our captain got the signal that it was a British ship. A few days later we landed at Madras harbour.

*

Isabelle Vaz narrates: 'We were fortunate to get onto one of the ships. One Mr Scindia helped us get berths. I remember sitting on the deck and eating a meal of boiled rice and cucumber pickled in vinegar and turmeric. We arrived Calcutta in one piece and, soon after, went to live in the family home in Nachinola, in the Bardez sub-district of Goa.'

*

Donald Menezes writes: 'Singapore had now fallen, and the fall of Rangoon and Burma became a strategic certainty. Evacuation to India was the common goal of all Goans, Anglo-Indians, Anglo-Burmese and Indians. But the Japanese held command of the seas. Fortunately they never sank any refugee boats and those who went by sea escaped all the hardships of the land trek. Most of us however declined the obvious risk.

'Our family decision was to move upcountry to Mawlaik on the Upper Chindwin River, to be with my uncle, Dr Victor D'Cruz, but my brother Robert elected to go by sea to Akyab on the Arakan coast, where our father was headmaster of the government school. From the beginning of hostilities, we three Menezes children, Robert, Donald and Muriel, studying at Rangoon University, had been cut off from Akyab, where our parents and younger sisters, Noreen and Patsy, were.

'Robert took ship at Rangoon on the eve of its fall. His aim was to go to the aid of our parents in Akyab, in the south. Along with him were several Akyab boys. As they boarded their ship, the sirens wailed and the ship moved swiftly to midstream. Their luggage had to be abandoned on the docks. Their ship took them to Calcutta in India, then they took a train to Dacca in Bangladesh, intending to proceed to Chittagong and then back to Burma and Akyab. But at Dacca, a Bengali boy named Dutta coincidently spied my mother on a houseboat hanging out the washing. He shouted joyfully to her and announced that Robert had come with him. Then he rushed to the railway station, got hold of Robert before the train left, and brought him to a joyful reunion with his mother and younger sisters. Robert then took the family to their pre-arranged destination, Nagpur, in Central India, where the family of my father's eldest sister lived.'

*

Patricia Duarte Van Camp remembers the sadness she felt when 'it became clear that our days in Rangoon were over. We had to look for a way to get out of the country. We, of course, were very lucky to have family abroad, my mother's Jewish family as well as my dad's family. We decided to go by boat to India and stay at my dad's sister's place in Bombay. As the story goes, we were able to leave Rangoon with the last boat that was able to get out without being bombed or torpedoed. But our home and my beloved piano was left behind and burned down, thanks to the "Scorched Earth Policy"—instead of handing over all valuables to the enemy, the entire block where we used to live was burned down so no one would be able to enjoy it!'

*

'Veronica Carvalho, who passed away recently, was a beautiful lady whom I admired for her vibrant and youthful personality. She told me of how she had to leave much of what she loved in Burma: 'As a young girl in Rangoon, I loved to attend the functions at the Goan Club which was known as Portuguese Club and had a great time dancing and socialising. I also have many other good memories of life in pre-war Burma. Playing tennis was the "in" thing at that time and as an impressionable twelve-year-old I recall carrying a tennis racquet around like an accessory when I travelled on buses, because it made me feel more attractive. I attended St. John's Convent, while my two brothers, Oscar and Vincent, were educated at St. Paul's Christian Brothers High School. We lived in Kyaikasan, in the suburbs of Rangoon, where my father had bought land and built a house. My father, Minguel Carmo Lobo, had migrated from India to Burma in the late 1920s. He had been sent by the Bombay Insurance Company to open a branch in Rangoon and he worked for this insurance company for many years.

'When the bombings continued, women and children were told to leave for India,' she says. 'My mother and I got berths on a ship to Madras. We were told not to carry any valuables, but my parents put our jewellery in a biscuit tin and we brought it out safely to India. On the ship, the place we were allotted was quite a distance from the lavatory, and every time I passed that way I made faces at a Chinese cabin boy. It's strange how I remember some details when so many others have slipped from my memory.'

'The late Mrs Especiosa D'Souza, known as Espy to her many friends, belonged to the large Filinto family from Calangute, Goa, some of whom I knew. Her daughter,

Mirna, wrote down her mother's story. Especiosa had good memories of Burma: 'My husband, Gilbert DeSouza, the youngest in his family, was eight years old when his eldest sister, Lizarda Beatson, took him from Sircaim (Bardez, in North Goa) to Moulmein (Lower Burma) where she had a hotel called Trevena for the British. She had five children from her first marriage to a Mr Pereira from Tivim who died and then she married an Englishman, Mr Beatson. Gilbert helped his sister and her family while he studied. His brother, Vincent, then started a confectionery-bakery called Milagrosa & Co. in Tavoy for him to manage, and they supplied the British Army with bakery items and newspapers. Vincent had his own book agency in Mergui also called Milagrosa & Co.

'Ours was an arranged marriage and Gilbert came down to Goa and we got married on May 19, 1941. After a month we left for Tavoy. I was there for six months and those were good days. We had a lot of Burmese and British friends and we were always served good food, I had good servants and cooks and enjoyed being a new housewife.'

When the war broke out she was pregnant. She says, 'We left Rangoon on February 7, 1942 and arrived in Calcutta on February 11th. The *SS Chilka* had Japanese prisoners on board and it was crowded. A Japanese plane bombed the ship next to ours. Whether they knew their men were on board or they meant to bomb us and missed, is a mystery. We were told to lie on our stomachs as the sirens went off, but we saw the devastation on the other ship and it was terrible. We lost our Rolex watches, some of our gold, my wedding presents and clothing on the ship, as some looting went on in the chaos.

'We landed in Calcutta and left by train for Bombay and there my sister-in-law, Olinda, arranged for my delivery at Dr Patrao's. But my father came to Bombay and took us back to Goa. My husband Gilbert had been held up for a week in Castlerock for questioning as he said he had escaped the war in Burma. We were very worried about him till he was united with us.'

'In February 1942, Wilma Silgardo and five of her siblings were put on the *SS Chilka* which brought them to Calcutta. She remembers that when the ship docked in Calcutta some navy men threw oranges and tea in mud pots up to the people on the deck.

'Eric Menezes, who had just got his Meccano set, could recall his family joining the exodus to India: 'On the morning of January 27th or 28th, Daddy had gone to town for some work and also to draw some more money from the bank. Whilst in town, he later recounted, he visited the Consul for China whom he knew well and that gentleman was rather surprised that we were still in Burma. His frank advice was quite simple: get out by sea while there was still time and the means to do so. Daddy immediately called at the office of Jemal & Co. who I think were the agents for BISN (British India Steam Navigation Co). Mr Jemal also knew Daddy very well and recommended a quick departure, the sooner the better, and went even further to write out a "passage order" for four persons on the *SS Chilka* which was scheduled to sail from Rangoon BISN Jetty at 5 p.m. that very evening for Visakhapatnam and Madras.

'It was now about noon, but pocketing the passage order,

he once again went to the bank and withdrew another five hundred rupees, which was then the maximum one could draw at a time, and raced back to Kokine. I remember him tearing down into the driveway at about 1.30 p.m. We children had finished lunch and, although young at that time, I felt the turning point had arrived when he announced to Mummy: "Pack up! We are leaving." Mummy's reaction was understandably one of surprise and shock and I remember clearly her first exclamation was: "And we leave all this?" To which Daddy's reply, down-to-earth as usual, was, "How many thousands is all this worth? Can it compare with the lives of our family?"

'There was no answer to this of course, and hastily two suitcases were pulled out and the feverish packing began; but such was the excitement and confusion that she omitted to put in even a single tin of milk powder, which we would need so badly during the sea voyage, though we had cartons of the stuff lying in the store room. It was just a question of cramming in whatever clothes came to hand without thought as to ultimate utility. I managed to slip in my boxes of lead soldiers and the Meccano set, as also most of the Hornby train set. In the middle of this, one of our guests suggested that as it was unsafe to carry jewellery, it could be left behind. Mummy's indignation can be imagined and she retorted angrily that if the ship was sunk, the gold should go down with her.

'The Austin was loaded and we left the house at Kokine, friends and all, and drove down to the Rangoon town house. It was only about 3.30 p.m. but the city was dull and silent with very few people moving around. The house was intact but the question was what to take. Daddy dug out a large bedroll and Mummy started stuffing it with household linen for use in Goa when we landed there. Finally within half-an-hour, the bulging bedding was strapped and loaded into the car. The flat was locked and then just abandoned. It was strange that one did not feel very much the fact that we were leaving behind material goods accumulated over a period of more than a decade. The streets were deserted and the drive to the steamer jetty was a short one.

'Fortunately the embarkation was orderly and we and our baggage were installed in the space reserved for us on the officer's accommodation deck. Meanwhile, some hundreds of other refugees were taken into the holds or given spaces on the cargo decks. All loading was completed and the vessel sailed on time at 5 p.m. As the sailing time will indicate, it was late afternoon and hazy, a derelict city in the background and the riverbank with a few dead bodies stranded in the mud. There must have been more floating in the river but my attention was fixed more on the city that was gliding by—first the Port Trust gardens where we used to play as children and listen to the police band playing light music, the cargo jetties and further down the river, Syriam and the Burma Oil Company oil tanks and then heading down the Irrawaddy River to the sea. Burma was becoming more distant and it gave me a sense of relief. It took the ship a little over an hour to clear the river mouth and head southwest towards the setting sun and India, which to every mind was safety. The voyage of course took about three days with a certain amount of risk always present.

'Now to get back to our surroundings. There must have been over a thousand refugees on board, mostly accommodated in the cargo holds, but with quite a number on the open decks. The *SS Chilka*, so far as I can remember, was a three-island vessel, with a raised forecastle, a middle section which housed the officers' quarters and some crew, the dining and recreation rooms and the navigating bridge. There was also a wide lifeboat deck with two lifeboats on each side and the officers' cabins with the saloon and pantry in between. We could not be given a cabin and the best the agency could do was to provide us a sheltered space with a canvas awning on the top and a canvas screen along the railings. They provided us with two mattresses, pillows and sheets. Compared to the conditions of the other refugees it was almost heavenly. Best of all, we were allowed the use of one toilet inside the officers' accommodation and the chief steward had apparently been instructed to provide us with any food that could be spared after the officers had been served. We got an average of one meal a day, usually dinner, which used to be brought to us on a tray whilst there was still daylight (before 6 p.m.). The rest of the meals were invariably coarse boiled rice and a watery dal. But on three or four occasions during the voyage, the steward slipped us a can of sardines and once a large tin of Crosse and Blackwell herrings in tomato sauce, which was a feast indeed. It was funny how these items, which were hardly looked at in the days of plenty, now became mouth-watering delicacies. The worst shortage was that of milk for my younger brother. The ship did not have much to give and I remember that one of the deck refugees gave Daddy a bottle of Horlicks which saved the day. Of course, Daddy replaced the bottle immediately once we landed at Visakhapatnam, but it was indeed kind of them to part with the bottle in the first place.

'No lights were allowed after sunset as a strict blackout

was observed. The voyage itself was uneventful, and I spent the time exploring the ship and peeping down into the great engine room with its glowing furnaces and shiny piston rods going up and down. Otherwise, I would watch the smoke issuing out of the funnel and streaming behind us in the wind and hope that the coal supply would not run out before we reached India. There was a ladder going up to the bridge from near our space, and it was a special treat to be allowed up to see the gleaming brass instruments and the officer on duty giving instructions to the sailor at the big steering wheel. There were also two sailors looking all around with their binoculars, maybe watching for submarines, and sometimes the ship would zigzag a little. Bedtime was early and the only entertainment was to see some red sparks coming out of the funnel.

'After three days of sailing, the first indication that we were approaching land was the sight of fishing coracles floating on the sea. These were Tamil fishermen, and soon the Indian coast became visible. It was a wonderful sight and at about 11 a.m. we entered Visakhapatnam harbour and docked. The first thing to do was to check in at a small hotel and the next was to visit the nearest church, where my parents fell on their knees in thanksgiving.

'As we were about to begin our lunch, the air-raid sirens began to wail. Mummy began screaming, thinking that we were destined for another bombing after coming all this way and, based on experience, she shouted at people to take shelter. No one seemed bothered and life continued as normal. We were then told that it was just a practice air-raid warning. Goa—and home—was just a train journey away and Daddy booked our tickets for the evening train.'

*

Before the airports in different parts of Burma were bombed systematically and taken over by the Japanese, some people managed to escape by plane. Felicity Fernandes remembers that suddenly, one day, there was a lot of hurrying and scurrying and packing being done. 'Mum, the five of us, ranging between six months and eight years, and our uncle, who was allowed to leave with us because of his bad eyesight, were rushed to the airport and loaded on to a cargo plane leaving for Calcutta. Dad had to stay behind as only women and children were being evacuated first.

'Mum told us later that one of their English friends had been told that the war was likely to continue for quite a while and she should warn her friends to leave without fail. She very kindly arranged the ticket—just a small piece of white paper which was headed "Air Permit for evacuation" and on which was typed: "This permit entitles Mrs F. Rodrigues and five children to travel by air from Shwebo under the Government Voluntary Evacuation Scheme. The cost of the fare Rupees seven hundred only has been credited into the Treasury." Also written, by hand, were the words "Details of children—two infants. Three under 10 years." It was dated March 26, 1942 and signed by one C.B. Pearson, then holding the post of Commissioner, F.S.S. and countersigned by one J.C. Paulton. This I found after Mum's death, in a small box containing all her important documents.

'In those times, if Mum had a weakness, it was for hats! In Burma, in those good old days, all the fashionable ladies wore hats, and not just for Sunday Mass. Mum had quite a collection of them which she kept in a black, round hatbox. She told us later that she didn't mind leaving behind her clothes, which in any case she couldn't have worn in Goa because of the heat, but she just couldn't part with her hats—some delicately trimmed with flowers and others with feathers or lace. As only one piece of luggage was allowed, all the children wore about three or four outfits—one over the other—and she and Uncle Alex did likewise, so that we all looked like little Santas. The hatbox was the only baggage that accompanied us. I am now the proud owner of this piece of our past. Incidentally, when we were in our teens, my sister Bridget and I wore those hats on Sundays till, to our great regret, Rome decreed it was no longer imperative for women to cover their heads at Mass.

'However, besides the hats, the box did also contain many other useful articles, like pencils, pens, rubbers, penknives, torches, playing cards, peg measures, bottle openers and even small tools which Dad and the boys and even my sister made good use of during their teens. My brother Ed used these tools in Australia and found them very handy there too!

'Mum was about twenty-five when we returned to India. She did not have much money—only what was in the shop at the time of our hurried departure, most of which, she told us later, had been stuffed in the bodies of two dolls, belonging to Bridget and me, which we carried very lovingly and carefully, unaware of their valuable contents.'

*

Leo Rego's father, Anthony Xavier Rego, married Anna Pelagia Dantas of Saligao before he migrated to Burma in search of greener pastures. He went to Moulmein in Lower Burma, where he got a job as bandmaster of the Police Band. As a side business, he also sold musical instruments at home. All their nine children—eight boys and one girl—were born in Moulmein. Leo and some of his family had the good fortune to get seats on an Allied plane, probably because his brothers, John and George, were in the British Army. They boarded the plane at Myitkyina airport and were among the refugees ferried across to Calcutta.

*

Myitkyina airport was the last to be bombed by the Japanese. The account of the bombing as told by Colin McPhedran in *White Butterflies* is reproduced in Part II of this book.

Chapter 7

The Great Trek

Not everyone was lucky enough to get away by the few boats or planes that the British government had arranged to evacuate the mass of people to India. Europeans and Eurasians were given priority and many Goans passed off as Anglo-Indians because they were Christians who spoke English fluently and wore Western clothes. Some of them possessed Portuguese passports too. Many other Indians were denied berths on the ships and even some able-bodied young Goan men were not permitted to get on ships or planes with other family members. The fragmentation of families added to the insecurity and uncertainty. The fear factor was intense as more bombings by Japanese planes created panic and pandemonium. So, thousands decided to walk across the border to India rather than face the dread of living under Japanese rule in Burma.

They had to obtain permits from the camp-in-charge and go in groups. The routes were unmapped and known only to the indigenous people who lived in the area. One route was across the Chindwin River, via Kalewa and Tamu to Imphal. There were two routes. The 'white route'—the easier, shorter route—was mainly for the British and some

Anglo-Indians. Most Indians were given permits to use the 'black route' which was more difficult and did not have many camps on the way. Another route, far north through the Hukawng Valley to Ledo, was a longer, much more risky one, and hundreds died on the way. This route was used by many people who had come to get on the plane at Myitkyina, the last functioning airport just before it was bombed, and by Indians who were not given permits for the Kalewa–Imphal route. A few Indians also made it from Arakan District to Chittagong in present-day Bangladesh.

Various survivors tell of the lack of a systematic plan for civilian evacuation. The Government of British Burma failed to provide proper estimates of people in transit and the British Government of India did not make adequate arrangements to assist the refugees. Along the way, local people and civilian volunteers provided food packets and helped some of the groups of trekkers through transit camps. At the camps on the 'white route' the refugees were given some fresh food, medicines and shelter for the night. But they could not stop there for long as the next group would be on its way to rest at the camp.

It was a hard trek over the mountains. Not only was the terrain rough and inadequately mapped, but the jungle was malarial and full of leeches, snakes and wild animals. Fear, hunger and sickness tested their physical and mental endurance to its limit. It is not known exactly how many hundreds lost their lives.

Those that survived were ravaged by disease and starvation. Many suffered from extreme weakness and could not continue the journey. No one could stop to bury the dead and even family members had to be left wherever they lay down to die. Survivors had to walk through the stench of bloated, decaying bodies. In spite of the physical hardships and the mental suffering, people survived to tell the story of the trek.

*

A.J. D'Cruz has written a record of the ordeal he and his family members went through during the trek. 'For some time, we believed the war would end soon, but as the days and months passed, we found, however that it was a real conquest of Burma. The Japanese bombed and took every town and township. When they took Mandalay and were planning to take Monywa, there was no more safety for us; so I decided to evacuate to India.

'I registered myself and all my children to proceed to India in the next convoy used for Europeans. Within a few days, the evacuation officer turned up in the morning and said that the convoy was leaving at 11 a.m. that day, and if we wanted to go with the family we had better get ready and be at the steamer docks by 10.30 a.m. No further enquiries were made as to who was going to pay our passages or what we would get to eat during the journey. All we were concerned about was to get away safely. We left by the steamboat and arrived at a place called Yuwa at 6 p.m., where a camp was established and arrangements for accommodation and food were made by the government.

'We slept there soundly and were detained for two days for want of transport to carry us further.

'The following morning, about sixty evacuees who were at the head of the list were picked out and sent further, in poling boats. My daughter-in-law, Ida, was eight months pregnant and in a bad state of health. When I found that she was not included among those leaving, I got alarmed as there was no help in case she got ill in the jungle, so I explained that to the camp evacuation officer. To our good luck, there were two European ladies who were professional nurses and were also evacuating. I begged of them to let my daughter-in-law also share their boat. When they were told that she was Mrs Cruz, the Civil Surgeon's wife, they told me that they would take her and attend to all her needs. They took her in their boat which left Yuwa that same day. I left after two days in a similar boat and was told at some camps where I stayed that the Europeans nurses carried my daughter-in-law in a chair from the boat up to the camp because she could not climb. I believe on arrival at Imphal, Ida took bad, and had to be taken to the state hospital. When the doctor said there was no danger, they took her to Bombay and gave her over to her parents there.

'As mentioned earlier, for want of transport we were detained at Yuwa for two days. After that, boats were brought and the remaining evacuees left at 7 a.m., four in each boat. Between Yuwa and Hlezeik, a distance of thirty-five miles, the poling boats took three days. Camps were provided by the government at stages of twelve miles each and in these camps, sleeping accommodation, dining rooms, and drinking water, boiled and cooled, were provided. On arrival at each stage we were served with a cup of tea and then a plateful of rice and dal twice a day at noon and at night. This was sufficient to keep our bodies and souls together. Moreover, we did not have to worry ourselves about food. It was cooked and served to each one.

'Now I am giving the names of family members who left

with me. They were: myself, Winnie, Emily, Arnold, Donald, Muriel and Bertram.

'After completing the thirty-five-mile journey, we arrived at Hlezeik. Here a comfortable camp was made on a high plateau and we remained there for three days. After that, we had to get onto the Kalewa–Tamu road, a distance of twelve miles only. For the first five miles we walked through a thick forest, but the next seven miles was open country without any shade. All the young people walked away, leaving my poor self behind. I was seventy-four years old at that time. I walked and walked in the hot sun from 11 a.m. to 4 p.m. till my knees started giving way and I could not use my legs anymore. The others left me far behind. I sat down near a small watercourse which had some water running, under the shade of a small tree. After some time, a gentleman named Lewis, a missionary of the Church of England, belonging to our party, happened to pass by and asked me why I was seated there. When I told him that I could not walk anymore, he stood on the road and waited till a truck laden with bamboo came up from Kalewa. He stopped the truck and put me by the side of the driver and told him to take me to Tamu. It was only a distance of three or four miles. I told the driver to drop me at the Tamu hospital. He did so and when the doctor-in-charge came and questioned me, I told him who I was and he took me to his house and gave me tea and biscuits and took me to the Tamu camp in his car.

'At Tamu, we were detained for six days for want of coolies. On the fourth day, the camp officer, Mr Atkinson, said that he could not feed us any longer as the camp shelters were required for new evacuees who were arriving at Tamu every other day. He picked out young persons to trek the country and in that list were Arnold, Donald and Emily. Muriel was suffering from malaria and Winnie could not walk on account of her foot, so these two were excluded. I volunteered to go with them but was not allowed to, because of my age. One Mrs Fernandes, an Arakanese lady, wife of a telegraph official, appealed to Mr Atkinson that she would not be able to walk those many miles carrying her partially crippled nine-year-old son and asked to remain till a doolie was secured. Mr Atkinson told her in reply to throw the boy into the jungle.

'Finally, after six days, we left Tamu at 5 p.m. and reached the first stage at about 9 p.m. Here we had rice and dal and slept. I must state here that on account of my old age and Muriel's fever, we were given one doolie which we used when needed. The journey was uphill, one hill after another, and at one stage our camp was pitched up on the top of a hill, and it looked as if I could touch the moon at midnight when I got out of bed. The following morning, we started very early and after completing two stages of about twelve miles each, we reached the highest point. I noticed two sign boards which said, "To Palel" and "To Tamu". We had left Tamu and would now go to Palel.

'Here, word was brought to me that my Winnie was down the road and could not walk. I sent my doolie to bring her up and paid the men Rs. 2. The next journey of two miles was downhill; we did it in two days and arrived at a village. Here we bought a goat kid and had a good meal after many days. When we were nearing Manipur state, our pathway was blocked by landslides and we had to climb up other hills to find new paths. Finally, we found that bulldozers were at work and had made new roads leading to Manipur.

We also came across empty jeeps and trucks going towards Palel, so we asked the military drivers for lifts.

'At last, we found ourselves in Palel, where it was raining continuously and we spent the night there. The following morning, we were conveyed to Imphal in motor buses. We remained here for three days. Mrs Shaw, the lady in charge of the camp, was very kind; she gave us substantial food consisting of meat, side dish, soup, curry and rice, pudding served free of charge and also clothing for both men and women. She was really good and motherly. We were very sorry to learn that a few weeks after we had left, the Japanese bombed the Imphal camp, killing fifty evacuees and Mrs Shaw with them.

'From Imphal we were driven to Dimapur, a railway station 120 miles away, by motor bus. We arrived late at night and were served a good meal. Here I came to see letters written by my Emily and Arnold stuck to the board in the dining chamber. The entire camp was flooded as it had rained the whole day. That same night, we boarded the train and left Dimapur. We met two gentlemen who had come from Akyab, at the railway station; they gave me news of my daughter Sophie and her husband.

'The following day, we arrived at Gauhati where the ladies—tea planters in charge of the camp—were very hospitable and supplied us with tea, coffee, plantains and biscuits. We proceeded further and crossed the Brahmaputra in a beautiful river steamboat and arrived at Parbatipur. We stayed the whole day here, left at night and arrived at Sealdah the following night at 12 a.m. From Sealdah station, we were taken to Loretto House where all the Burma evacuees were accommodated.'

*

A.J. D'Cruz's grandson, Donald Menezes, who was a lively teenager at that time, writes about his experiences of the trek quite matter-of-factly and without any self-pity. 'Meanwhile, as the Japanese advance continued up Central Burma the order was given for evacuation of Upper Burma. So we prepared for the Great Burma Trek through jungle and mountain, the route by which half-a-million people returned to India, with thousands perishing on the way.

'One day before the trek started, we heard a strange rumbling sound and our house on a low hill shook as in an earthquake. Looking out of our windows, we saw about forty elephants marching past, with European women and children perched upon their howdahs. They were the families of the forest officers of the Bombay Burma Trading Co., which was evacuating its staff.

'On April 7, 1942, we moved, as evacuation started on the "white route". Up river we went by paddle-wheeler, and then disembarked at Ywa, a bamboo-and-mat river camp in the midst of dense jungle. At Ywa a mountain stream empties into the Chindwin River. The whole Chindwin valley is inhabited by Chins, an ethnic tribe that looked somewhere between Chinese, Tibetan and Burmese. For three days in Ywa, we enjoyed the delights and hardships of jungle life.

'On April 10th, we embarked at early morn on a convoy of small river boats, and were poled upstream along this swift mountain stream. We struggled up a series of rapids in a narrow valley between steeply rising and thickly forested hills, the scenery magnificent and the air cool and bracing. The forests were alive with parrots and other colourful jungle birds and monkeys. Sometimes we saw the pugmarks of tigers near our camps. We set out every morning at seven, breaking for a lunch consisting of dal, rice and Japanese sardines, and then pushed on so as to reach a government camp by sunset, where a hot dinner of unvarying dal, rice and sardines awaited us.

'Towing our boats up the rapids was a thrilling experience. We were handed tow-ropes attached to the bows and sides of the boats and wading waist or chest deep, climbing, slipping and sliding on rocks amidst cascading water, we hauled the boats upstream over the rapids. The boatmen manoeuvred the boats, holding the bows straight against the onrushing white water by pressing with their poles against the rocks. It was dangerous work. But it kept us in high spirits. Playing with danger always gives one a high.

'Our first night halt on the stream was at Yenan, an abandoned oil camp on petroleum oil fields. We had barely settled down to sleep in our bungalow, when we heard a commotion and shots at the water's edge. We became alarmed. Was this an attack by armed dacoits? Such attacks had been reported. We pushed the women and children to inner rooms and took up positions near the doors. Two had revolvers; the rest had sticks. After a while, we heard reassuring shouts and laughter and we relaxed. It had turned out that a party of boatmen returning downstream espied their compatriots and decided to camp beside them. Our Gurkha guard ordered the leading boatman to stop, fearing they were dacoits. Seeing him unarmed but still advancing, the Gurkha threw down his rifle and leapt on the man's chest with both boots. Immediately the other boatmen rushed up with their steel-spiked poles. Upon this, the second Gurkha guard fired warning shots and the whole camp sprang up in alarm. At this point, it was the presence of mind of one

The Great Trek

Krishna, a dark and dashing hunter, that saved the situation. Son of a Burmese mother and a millionaire Tamilian father, he rushed into the middle of the developing fray shouting in Burmese and Hindustani and successfully averted bloodshed.

'The valley got greener, narrower and steeper as we moved up. At camp Telangya, progress by boat was no longer possible. The drop from one level to another was almost like a waterfall. It was indescribably beautiful, a perfect picnic spot, like the Hampshire Falls near Maymyo in the hill station where I was born. Between one rapid and the next, the water was like a large swimming pool, deep and quiet. I showed off my swimming with the few who could swim. Some of the Anglo-Indian and Anglo-Burmese girls looked gorgeous in their swimsuits. I echoed the sentiment of the Great Moghul in his summer palace in Kashmir: "If there is a heaven upon earth, it is here; it is here."

'No more boats now; we marched on foot. From camp Hlezeik we marched through a dry forest. Dry leaves and twigs crackled underfoot. High overhead, the trees arched as if forming a great Gothic cathedral. Then we hit the road to Tamu, the last town on Burma's border with India. The road ended at Tamu. The lack of a road link with India proved a strategic weakness in the war.

'One branch of the Kalewa–Tamu road was known as the "black route" and thousands of Indians perished on this route from typhoid, cholera, dysentery and other illnesses. My uncle, Dr Victor D'Cruz, Chief Medical Officer for the route, had not only to attend to the dying but even to personally bury the dead. People were afraid to touch the corpses for fear of contagion. But my uncle was a tough leathery officer inured to death and suffering.

'As cars and trucks passed us on the road, they threw up clouds of choking dust that added to the discomfort of our parched throats and dry nostrils. By one of the road culverts, I saw a stagnant pool. I was desperate for water, and the pool looked cool and inviting. I knew the risks, but I parted the vegetation and drank the cool water. It tasted like the nectar of the gods. But for years subsequently, I suffered severely from cerebral malaria. Of course I could have got malaria from mosquito bites too.

'Tamu, a town in northwest Burma on the border with what today is Manipur in India, was then a graveyard of abandoned cars, trucks and buses. A coolie strike was on for higher wages and smaller backpack loads. The camp reached overflow point and separated families caught up with one another. Then the Commandant ordered the able-bodied to move on, carrying whatever they wanted on their backs. My sister Muriel was flat on her back with acute malaria, so my grandfather who was allotted a doolie—a stretcher carried by four coolies—gave it up to her. But they did not move till the strike ended.

'Meanwhile, an Akyab boy and his sister, Agnes Fernandes, asked my help to carry his large radio set. In the process we lost the tail-end of our party and found ourselves following an Indian party, going on an altogether different route. As the light failed we halted, knowing we were lost. And the night was soon upon us. Suddenly, Agnes, who was chirping like a sparrow, panicked. She began to cry hysterically. It had at last dawned upon her that the jungle was not only full of wild animals but also of dangerous two-legged ones. Visions of rape and murder came upon her. But we men took charge. We had to play it cool. We told her quietly and firmly to "shut up".

'A faint moonlight peeked through the trees and the surrounding gloom. The night was silent except for the occasional squawk of a bird, the chatter of a monkey or the grunt of a jackal.

'Half-an-hour later, providentially, we heard the lowing of bulls and the creak of wheels. It was a party of Chin cartmen homeward bound for Tamu. Quickly, we explained our situation, and they readily took us back to Tamu on their carts. The camp Commandant was furious when we got back and gave us a severe scolding. He ordered us to move out first thing in the morning. At daybreak, we set out again, but only after throwing away the radio that had caused all the trouble and by midday, we reached Camp Middleton. Some members agreed to take us to our original party who were still there and they were glad to see that we were safe. They had had a mishap. A young woman attempted a shortcut over a hill. An Indian guard on the road, seeing her, tried to molest her. But when he put his hand over her mouth, she bit his finger to the bone and would not let go. The man finally broke free and fled. He was later caught and punished. But the girl was badly shaken and had to rest.

'After lunch, I raced on and caught up with Aunt Emily and Arnold. They were so glad to see me safe and hear of my adventure. Up hill and down dale we raced until we heard the sound of bulldozers and crashing trees. From the top of the hill, we saw the red gash of a road on the next green hill, where the Indian Army engineers were pushing a road through the jungle. We soon met the engineers, who warmly welcomed us. They put us on empty trucks and sent us on to their base at Palel, in Manipur. At sundown we arrived at Palel, were given a hot meal and shown our billets in a cattle shed. It was the height of the hot season, but because of the elevation of Manipur, the weather was cold. At night we were glad to cover ourselves with straw to keep warm.

'The next day, buses transported us to Imphal, capital of Manipur, which is a kind of Shangri-la in the hills, with a quaint old civilization, a well-organised market and beautiful handicraft industries. The people appeared to be a mixture of Bengali and Burmese. Here was an ample supply of clothing and blankets collected by the Red Cross and made available to the Burma refugees.

'After two or three days, we were again transported by buses over high mountains and dangerous roads to the Indian railhead at Dimapur in the Assam valley. After a night in camp, a train took us to Pandu on the mighty Brahmaputra, a river which bears a rare male name and means "son of Brahma" in Sanskrit.

'We crossed the river in a magnificent ferry, with a splendid bar, all shiny brass work and sparkling glassware. It was built to suit the lifestyle of the Assam tea planters. The ferry had just brought up a contingent of Indian troops, who were moving to the front. The mustachioed officers, with their swords, turbans, revolvers and Sten guns, looked magnificent. The Brahmaputra, one of the major rivers of Asia, looked like an immense sea, with the orb of the sun sinking down into it. A feature of the crossing were the "manatees" [river dolphins] that leapt twenty feet out of the water and plopped back into it. These water animals resembled fat pigs, only bigger. On the other side was Amingaon, a tidy riverside town. From there, the train raced to Calcutta on the Indian Railways broad-gauge railway. We arrived in Calcutta around midnight. The Great Burma Trek was over. It was April 30, 1942. It had lasted three weeks.'

*

Thelma Menezes was pregnant with her first child when she made the trek. 'When Monywa came under enemy threat, we registered our names for evacuation. The British government had organised an overland route with camps, predominantly for Europeans, Anglo-Indians and Anglo-Burmans.

'We boarded a paddle streamer with our luggage and went up the Chindwin River. It was a sad sight to see dead bodies floating past, victims of epidemics on the "black route" for Indians. We were advised to add potassium permanganate crystals to river water before drinking.

'At Mawlaik, the next stop, we met Anthony John D'Cruz and his family. After Mawlaik, the river narrowed and we went in small paddleboats, which had to be towed or poled across swift rapids by the boatmen while we walked on rocky banks. For ten days, we went from camp to camp, setting off early, stopping for a meal of rice, dal and tinned Japanese sardines, starting off again to reach the next camp before dark, where an identical meal awaited us. Throughout, we ate the same fare.

'The river trip ended at Kalewa and we proceeded on foot to Tamu. We had to carry our own luggage and extra stuff was "sold" to local villagers. Mrs Machado parted with her four Jacobean cut-glass tumblers for eight annas, while my husband's guitar fetched him ten. It was also here that my husband had to remain on essential service. We would wait for him in Calcutta.

'Beyond Tamu, it was rough going, through thickly forested mountainous terrain, infested with mosquitoes, believed to be the land of the Naga headhunters. We were given strict instructions to stay together and to keep pace, reaching the next camp before sunset. One strayed at one's own risk. At Camp Middleton, we heard Emily D'Cruz sing "Alice Blue Gown". Her voice soared beautiful and clear in the still of the night. It was a welcome break.

'The walk continued for twelve to fifteen miles a day to the Indian border, then in trucks manned by retreating American troops, through Imphal to Dimapur and by train to Calcutta and the refugee camp at Loreto Convent. It was the end of the trek, which had taken nearly a month. Ours was the twenty-third convoy, the last to get through. The twenty-fourth was bombed and evacuation stopped.'

*

Thelma's husband's uncle, Leonard Menezes, who was a headmaster in Tavoy, did not make it. Staying behind on essential duty, he missed all the outgoing flights and was forced to take the hazardous 350-mile trek through the Hukawng Valley in the north. Suffering from a weak heart, he collapsed on the route. His body was found by his students.

*

Sylvia D'Gama relates how her father and brother George, then seventeen years old, had to walk across the mountains to India with a group of ten people. Due to the monsoons, some shorter routes became inaccessible and they had to take the longer 350-mile route. 'I was told that they suffered fatigue and hunger and, to make matters worse, George got severe diarrhoea. There was no medicine and George became so weak that he could not walk. Each person was struggling with his own problems and no one could afford to stop or help George along. He told my father to leave him behind and continue walking; otherwise both of them would be left in the jungle to die. One can imagine how difficult it must have been for Dad to do that; but others pointed out that he had a responsibility to the rest of the family who were waiting for him in Calcutta. So, very reluctantly he left George sitting and leaning against a tree while he walked on with the group.

'George was resigned to facing death. Some time later, a Naga woman happened to come that way. The moment she saw him, for some reason, she ran back down the hill. George had heard stories of Naga headhunters, and maybe it was a misguided notion, but he thought that she had gone back to bring the menfolk to eat him alive. He was terrified, and the surge of fear was so strong that it forced him to his feet and he ran for his life. From then on, he started walking. What an ordeal he must have gone through, alone in the dense jungle, without food or water! He walked for days, observing the monkeys and eating whatever he saw them eat. One day he saw hundreds of beautiful butterflies in a certain spot. He looked around expecting to see a lot of flowers in this area but what he saw horrified him. The butterflies were covering a bloated corpse and they must have been feasting off the juices that oozed from the decaying body. He just fled from the scene!

'Somehow, he reached Dibrugarh hospital, where he was treated for his illness and taken care of in every way. Our parents were informed of his whereabouts and it was like a miracle for all of us. Dad had offered masses for his soul when he got to Calcutta, but my mother had refused to attend the masses because she felt George was still alive. He was later brought to Calcutta and was cured of the diarrhoea. He went on to join the British Army and was posted to the Middle East.'

*

Lena Rego also went through the experience of having to leave a family member behind when they evacuated to India by ship. She recalls, 'My mother was very worried about my brother Lucas who had been left behind in Rangoon and cried all the time for him. When one lady told us how her son who had also stayed back in Rangoon was cut into pieces, put in a sack and thrown in the river by the Japanese, my mother could not take it anymore and had a nervous breakdown. There was no news of Lucas for a long time, till one day a letter arrived. My mother would not allow anyone to open and read it. So my father placed the letter on the altar and when she was calmer he opened the letter and read that Lucas was in the camp in Chunar, in North India, together with our cousins.

'When he was reunited with us, he told us how he worked for the Japanese in Rangoon but a Japanese officer for some reason thought he was working for the British and chased him with a sword. While running away from him, Lucas tripped on a stone and the officer tried to cut off his neck with the sword but instead wounded him on the shoulder. After that, Lucas decided to walk across to India. He told us about the tough times he went through. During the day the sun was so hot but they would shiver during the cold nights. While walking through the thick jungle, some people were eaten by wild beasts and many died of snakebite too. Some just died in their sleep and some never got up when they fell while walking. Lucas became very weak and exhausted. Some food was dropped by Allied planes, but most of the time people walked on an empty stomach. We felt so sorry for him and all the others who went through so much suffering.'

*

Felicity Fernandes recalls, 'Dad, along with a great many others, decided to trek it to India over the Mizo Hills, which are in the Northeast, between India and Burma. It was a tough trek. Dad witnessed the death of a number of his friends and colleagues on the way. He said they would put up camp at night and leave early the next morning, only to hear later that the previous camp had been bombed soon after they had left. Some drowned while crossing the Chindwin River, others died of malaria, jaundice, cholera, hunger and thirst. My brother Ed recalls being told by Dad that they were even chased and bitten by dogs, and he remembers being shown the scars behind Dad's knees. As they trekked along, most of them had to leave behind their precious possessions since they had no strength to carry them across the border.

'Dad's brother, Wenceslaus, and his wife, Maggie, with two very young children, Adilia, around one year old and Hedwig, about three months old, also joined the trek. Aunt Maggie later told us that they travelled by bullock-cart all the way and her greatest regret had been to leave her precious sewing-machine behind. Fortunately, the close friend with whom she had left it brought it to Mumbai later.

'Once across the India border, Dad and all the survivors were helped along the way with food, clothing and shelter, till he arrived in Goa where he was treated for jaundice. As soon as he had rested and regained his strength, he went to Mumbai and got a job as chief accountant with a well known company named G. Kader and Sons, who were builders, painters, shipwright contractors and commission agents.'

*

Veronica Carvalho's father and brothers too could not get on the ship that she and her mother sailed on and they had no choice but to make the trek. 'They brought along our dogs,' she remembers. 'My father told us about the dangerous river crossings and the long dangerous walk. They carried wireless sets and used them sometimes. I know that both my brothers were in the Civil Service. Oscar had to hide in the jungles of northern Burma during the war. He later married a Burmese lady and lived in Burma. They visited India only once after that.'

*

Renee Pinto's father, Antonio Xavier Nascimento Rodrigues, was taken to Rangoon when he was fourteen by his sister Maria Piedade and brother-in-law Minguel Caitan Pinto, who had a bakery there. He attended St. Paul's High School for three years and after that started working for the well-known pharmaceutical company E.M. D'Souza & Co. He made a trip to Goa in 1936 and married Eulalia D'Lima, after which he took her back to Maymyo where he had a little home above the chemist shop. It was here that his son Agnelo and daughter Renee were born. Renee was a baby when her mother took the trek with two small children. She knows of their experiences from the stories her mother told.

'After the routes by sea and air were blocked, people started walking. My father had to stay on in Burma but decided to send his family to Goa and trusted his friend,

Dr Ottoman, to take care of us on the way. So my mother, my elder brother Angelo and I joined the group of English people including Dr Ottoman and his family and we trekked through north Burma into Assam. Of course I remember nothing of this, being just an infant at that time. But my mother often told us about this long and difficult journey, walking and walking and going through so much physical and mental suffering, more so because she had two small children to take care of and there was no proper milk or water for us. Her anxieties only increased when she saw so many corpses of babies, who had died for lack of milk just lying by the roadside. But fortunately, we were travelling with Britishers so we got more food and medical supplies than the others did. There were porters to help carry us children and the luggage and sometimes we got rides on elephant back. Still, from what my mother narrated, it was a terrible ordeal for her but somehow they managed to reach Calcutta.'

*

Wilma Silgardo and five of her siblings had sailed to Calcutta, while her parents and youngest brother and sister were fortunate to get away in April by air. But her elder brother, Dr Olwen Silgardo, walked across with the British Army. Another brother, Romer, too had to trek the long difficult route to India. He was over twenty-one and could not get a seat on a ship or plane.

Despite the separation of families, with members having to travel out of Burma by different means, most of them made it to safety in India and were reunited after many anxious weeks and months.

Road sign showing distances to various cities in India and Burma

BURMA BEFORE THE SECOND WORLD WAR

Top: Scene at Dalhousie Park, Rangoon
Middle left: Sule Pagoda Road, Rangoon
Middle right: Old Rangoon from across the river
Bottom: Road sign at the Irrawaddy River

Top: Royal carriage going through a triumphal arch, Rangoon
Bottom: The Royal Hotel, Rangoon

Pre-War Portraits

Opp. page: An upper-class Burmese couple of the nineteenth century
Top: Shakuntala Peter's family

Top: Geraldine Pinto's family
Bottom: The Rodrigues family

Top: Thelma Menezes
Bottom: Kevin Pinto's family

Top: A.J. D'Cruz
Bottom: Outside D'Cruz house on 52nd Street, Rangoon

Top: Inside the hall of the D'Cruz house
Bottom: Outside D'Cruz house on 52nd Street, Rangoon

Top: Patricia Duarte's family
Bottom: Benegal Dinker Rao

War Comes to Burma

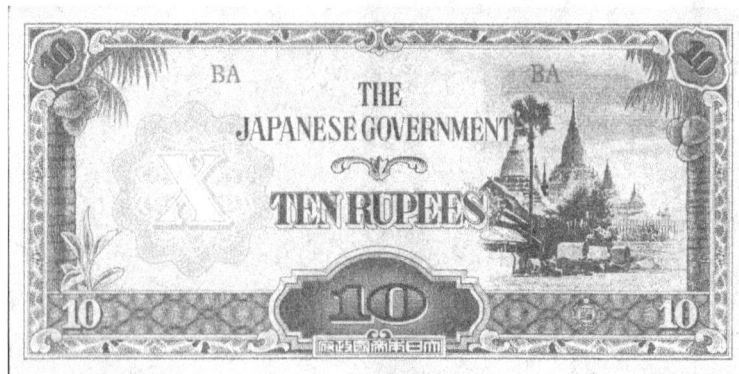

Invasion money issued by the Japanese during their occupation of Burma

Severe Bombing of Rangoon!

Imperial Army Headquarters News Flash

Dec. 24, 1941, 5:10 PM

Yesterday, on December 23rd, the combined Imperial Army Air Force heavily bombed the Rangoon Airport; Spitfire fighters (along with possible Buffalos) engaged the bombers in violent aerial battle. Ten fighters were shot down with others (an accurate count could not be determined); also, four fighter planes on the ground plus two bombers were hit and burned. Four of our planes did not return.

December 23, 1941, after navigating long distances, our combined army air force bomb wing severely bombed the Rangoon, the capital of Burma. On the same day, a second wave continued the attack in the afternoon. Then on the 25th, a third wave pressed on the attack, destroying 80 enemy planes. This severed the military's bloodline (meaning system), the bombing giving their harbor/bay group a fatal blow.

With the capitulation of Manila on January 2nd a turning point, the fierce air strategy was speeded up; on March 8th, with the capitulation of Rangoon, the air strategy has now started onto Mandalay and Lashio while considering losses.

Enemy fighter planes engaged our new advanced fighters but one after another, they were shot down, trailing black smoke.

The ground erupted from the heavy bombs; valuable buildings were instantly enveloped in heavy smoke as the city, pier and airport were consumed in fiery blazes.

Opp. page: Bombing of Rangoon on 23 December 1941 taken from a Japanese plane
Top: Japanese text on the back of the photo *(inset)*, with English translation sourced by Mustang Koji

Opp. page: Map showing routes used by refugees while leaving Burma
Top: Ava Bridge after being bombed during the Second World War

LEAVING BURMA

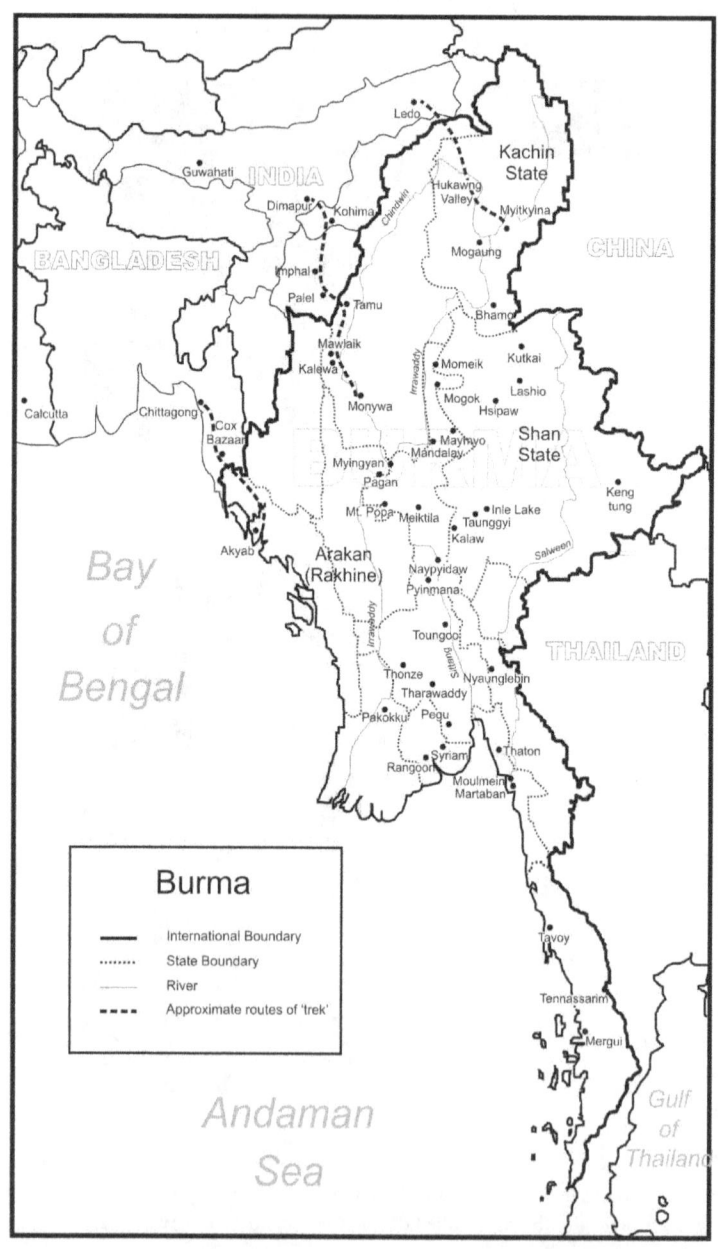

Evacuation /General Instructions, Taunggyi

Enquiries regarding evacuation were to be directed to:
Mrs Bruce Scott
Rev'd. H.R.L. Slater
Station Staff Officer

EVACUATION

GENERAL INSTRUCTIONS TO PROSPECTIVE EVACUEES

There is no Government Order that Women and Children are to evacuate, but expectant Mothers and Women with young children are strongly advised to take this opportunity of evacuating by Air to avoid any later rush though this may never become necessary. There is no present urgency on any other account.

The following gives a short précis of the Scheme for Evacuation to India:-

(1). By Air.   (2) By Road.

(1). AIR. The probable destination in India will be Calcutta or Chittagong. Women, Children and Invalids will be evacuated by this route.

FARES. will probably be Rs.280/- to Rs.330/- per adult, and Rs.140/- to Rs.165/- for Children under ten (Babies in arms free) according to destination. This must be paid in CASH by persons travelling. Necessitous cases if reported will be considered on their merits.

Priority. Will be strictly enforced
- (a) Expectant Mothers.
- (b) Mothers with Babies in Arms.
- (c) Mothers with Children under 10 Years.
- (d) Mothers with children over 10 and under 14 years.

Women, Invalids and old people of both sexes unable to stand the road journey to India. Women without children who are able to stand the journey by road will only be evacuated after the above four classes. The journey from Taunggyi to Mandalay will be arranged either by train or by car/lorry through this Headquarters. Sufficient food for the journey to Shwebo and when in Shwebo should be taken by parties. Baggage allowed by Air is 33lbs. for adult and 16lbs for child under 10. Excess will not be carried by Air. Passports if available will be taken.

(2). ROAD. CHINDWIN ROUTE.

- (a) by train to Monywa, from thence accommodation will be reserved on one of the I.F. Steamers for the party to Kalewa, Motor transport from Kalewa to Tamu may be possible if not journey by cart or on foot, and from thence to Palel organised parties of coolies, Elephant and bullock cart transport will operate. It is possible that as more of the road is finished this journey by foot will be shortened. The organisation includes provisioning and shelter at the different stages, simple food and water only will be provided. The able bodied will walk by easy stages, others will be transported by any means available.
- (b) The MAXIMUM baggage allowed is 60lbs. per head composed of bed-roll and one packege – mosquito net is MOST essential in the TAMU VALLEY. Included in the baggage allowance a small box of tinned foodstuffs should be taken which would be used for the party as a whole and not for individual consumption. Each Evacuee should take plate, knife, fork, spoon and a drinking mug. Soap, towel, iodine, bandage, Topi, boots or strong shoes and a

Evacuation /General Instructions, Taunggyi

water bottle are ESSENTIAL. It is also advised to carry a haversack or Shan Bag which would be used for small personal possessions. This, and any additional kit or belongings MUST of course be carried by the individual, as anything over the 60lbs. allowance will not be carried by the Organisation. Suitcases are NOT convenient and are heavy. Kit bags are much preferable as carrier loads. Food to make up the 60lbs. total – Cheese, Biscuits, dried milk, raisins, Oxo cubes, dried fruit, marmite, tinned food (with opener).

BRIEF DESCRIPTION OF JOURNEY. Train to Monywa Rest Camp, Steamer up Chindwin, Rest Camp, Walk from Camp to Camp in short stages to end of road, motor buses in India from Camp to Camp to Indian Railway Station, Rail to reception Base.

DISPERSAL. By train to destination in India. Cost. The arrangements are free of charge to final destination in India.

MEDICAL If you have a Medical Officer's Certificate for ☐noculated☐ bring it – if not you must be ☐noculated before starting.

SERVANTS. One servant per person only may be taken but if these are accepted they come under Convoy orders and must give service to the personnel of the Convoy in general.

CAMPS. Huts are erected – each camp has a staff who will prepare simple hot food and boiled water for water bottles.

CLOTHES FOR JOURNEY. Long sleeves and long slacks or other long clothes covering arms and legs should be worn as a protection day or night against mosquito and other bites.

PETS. NO pets may be taken.

APPLICABLE TO BOTH ROUTES. Evacuation and the method of evacuation will depend in part on physical fitness and general medical grounds. Intending evacuees are advised to keep themselves ready to move at short notice as it may be impossible to give any lengthy warning, and once times and dates are given no delay can be permitted. Any enquiries regarding evacuation can be directed to Mrs. Bruce Scott, The Rev. H.R.L. Slater or to the Station Staff Officer, Taunggyi. Intending evacuees by road are advised not to carry large sums of cash but it may be possible (uncertain) to obtain travellers cheques and those wishing to endeavour to obtain these will please apply to the Station Staff Officer, as soon as possible. Temporary arrangements will be made by the Government in India for those who have no private arrangements. Identity disc or label with name and destination in India if known will be worn. Label each package of baggage with a strong label.

Sgd. STATION STAFF OFFICER
S.D.
9/3/42
TAUNGGYI

Opp. page: Evacuation ID card for Frank Rodrigues
Top: Air evacuation ticket for the Rodrigues family
Bottom: One of the evacuation routes later used by refugees while leaving Burma

IDENTITY CARD

Signature
Or Thumb
Impression
Of Holder

PERMIT
TO
BOARD. No. 012484

Name FRANK RODRIGUES
Address of M/s. G. KADER & SONS,
Employer 133, SHERIFF DEVJEE ST.
Occupation ACCOUNTANT
Height 5'-4" Build SLIM
Permit valid to 30-6-46
Extended to ....
Extended to ....
Date of Issue 21-11-44

Dy. Commissioner of Police, Port.

NOTE. — This Permit is subject to any Notification issued under Defence of India Rules. Ships' Officers, owners and agents may refuse permission to board without assigning any reason.

FEDERATION OF INDIAN CHAMBERS OF COMMERCE AND INDUSTRY.
CENTRAL INDIAN EVACUEES RELIEF COMMITTEE.

Particulars of claim in respect of loss of moveable properties against the government of <u>Burma</u>.

PARTICULARS (B.)

SERIAL No.

In case of claim for loss of immoveable property reference to serial number in Register A.

NAME OF THE APPLICANT. DR (MRS) ROSE DUARTE.
(In block letters.)

ADDRESS OF THE APPLICANT. No: 77, N. I. LINES,
(In block letters.) KARACHI.

DATE OF RECEIPT OF APPLICATION.

Nature of moveable property lost to be indicated by reference to the number in the list hereunder.

	Rs.	As.	Ps.
Household furniture including crockery, utensils, etc, and Scheidmeyer piano Rs 2500	5619	0	0
Wearing apparel	400	0	0
Books, medical & surgical instruments	2500	0	0
Silver ware	200	0	0
VALUE OF THE PROPERTY LOST	Rs. 8719	0	0

8. Whether covered by ordinary or War Risks Insurance or by both, and if so for how much stating the name of the Company.

9. Name of the company and the number of its shares or debentures held and their aggregate value, the company having ceased to exist or function.

10. Place where the property was last kept. No: 10, 49th STREET RANGOON.

11. How the loss occurred, whether by enemy action, etc. or by reason of having to be abandoned for want of facilities for their removal. BY HAVING TO BE ABANDONED FOR WANT OF FACILITIES FOR THEIR REMOVAL.

12. Claim for whole or part of goods supplied to or shipped under the order of,

I declare that the above statement is correct to the best of my knowledge.

Dated .21-1-.43.... Signed Dr (Mrs) Rose Duarte.

List of moveable properties left or lost, to be indicated by number in column 6 above.

1. Household furniture including crockery, utensils, etc.
2. Wearing apparel and bedding.
3. Books. 4. Silver ware. 5. Jewellery 6. Motor Car. 7. Bicycle.
8. Cart. 9. Lorry. 10. Carriage. 11. Cargo boat. 12. Elephant.
13. Bullock. 14. Cow. 15. Stock-in-trade (to be named specifically)
16. Machinery, (to be particularised.) 17. Mill Stores, etc. 18. Timber.
19. Shop or office equipment. 20. Grains. 21. Crops. 22. Advances.
23. Outstandings. 24. Deposits with individuals, banks, firms, Government or quasi-Government bodies

These particulars will be filled up by the above Committee's office.

NOTE: After being copied in the Committee's Register, these particulars will be forwarded to the Government.

Claim forms for property and belongings left in Burma by refugees

Contributor Portraits

Top: Veronica Carvalho
Bottom: A.C. DeSouza

Top left: Especiosa D'Souza
Top right: Gerald D'Souza
Bottom: Patricia Duarte Van Camp

Felicity and Cyril Fernandes on their golden wedding anniversary

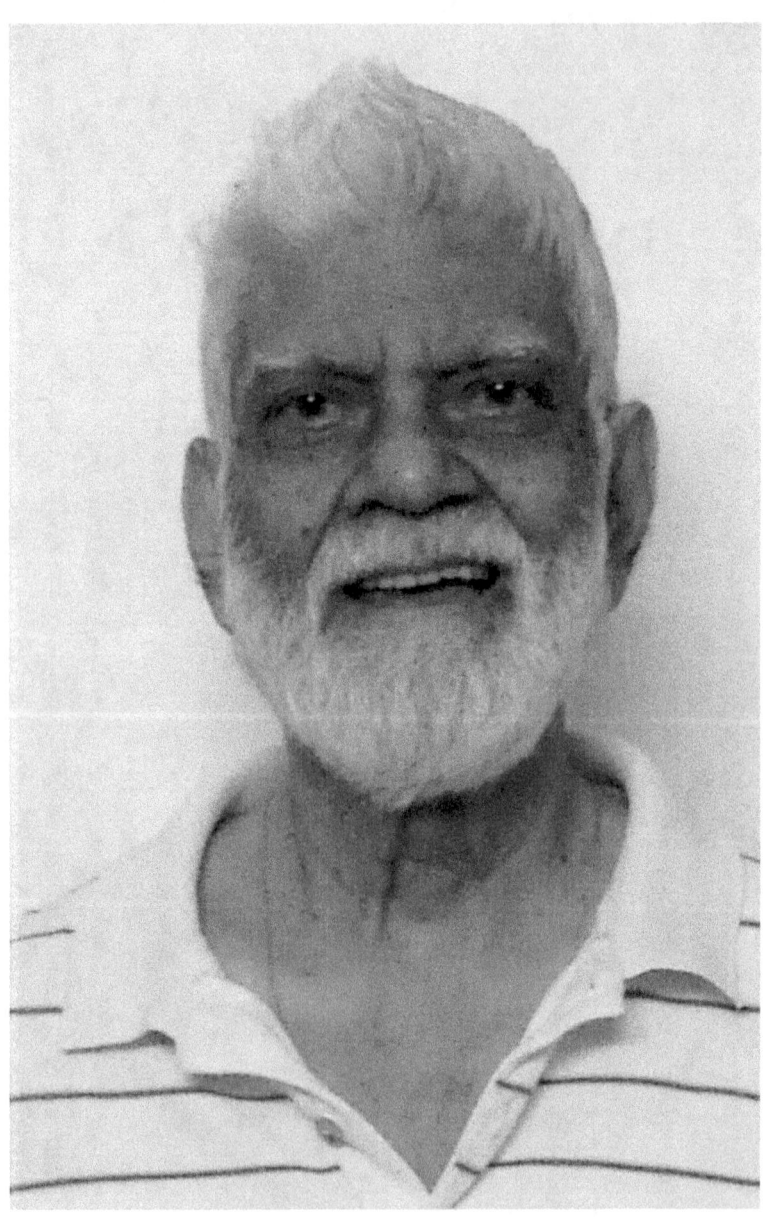

Tony Machado

Bottom: Eric Menezes
Opp. top: Donald Menezes with his sister, Patsy
Opp. bottom: Thelma Menezes

Opp. top: Hugh Nazareth
Opp. bottom: Gerry O'Connor
Top: Mrs Shakuntala Peter
Bottom: Geraldine Pinto and her sister, Matty

Top: Lena Rego
Bottom: Benegal Dinker Rao

Isabelle Vaz

Peter Vaz

Chapter 8

Surviving Japanese Rule in Burma

Many Indians, including Goans, tried to escape, but those who were unable to had no option but to try to survive in Japanese-occupied Burma. Some of them had horrifying tales to tell. During the three years of Japanese occupation, the people of Burma who had previously lived comfortable lives now faced untold economic hardships. Salt, oil, soap, clothing and medicines all but disappeared from the market. Even rice was rationed. As 'masters', the so-called 'liberators' occupied the best residences, took away medicinal stocks from hospitals, recruited forced labour whenever required, beat and slapped Burmese recruits in public and humiliated monks (even though they called themselves Buddhist). Many incidents of rape were also reported. Anyone who slightly resembled a European was caught and locked up in concentration camps. Stories were told about gruesome methods of torture: pulling out fingernails, putting salt on raw wounds, allowing water to fall drop by drop on the head until a hole was formed, pouring hot oil in the ear, and so on.

But there were also those who learnt to live with the Japanese and came through the war unscathed. Some of those who lived in Burma during the Japanese occupation were employed to work for the new masters. Some even experienced the human side of the Japanese officers and soldiers they came in contact with.

*

Nonagenarian Peter Vaz, who now lives in Saligao, Goa, India, is my paternal uncle. He is the only survivor of the seven Vaz brothers who repatriated from Burma in 1966 when the policies of the ruling military regime made it difficult for foreigners to continue living there. The family had gone through the Second World War and Japanese occupation in Burma.

Peter told me that he and his brother Anthony had escaped the first bombing of Rangoon where they were resident students at the Government Technical Institute in Insein, a nearby suburb. But he remembers going back to attend classes in January and February 1942 and they even sat for an examination. Bombings continued in central Rangoon but it was comparatively safer for them in Insein. However, in March they were sent home to Taunggyi. The institute bus took them for a part of the way and the rest of the journey, a distance of about 280 miles, was made with great difficulty through war-stricken Burma. Taunggyi and the Southern Shan State were no longer refuges for the Vaz family. They experienced bombing by Japanese planes in April 1942, more than four months after the first bombing of Rangoon. Peter tells the story of how the Vaz family survived three years of Japanese occupation in Burma.

'I recall it was Market Day in Taunggyi* when the air-raid siren sounded. All of us who were at home ran into the

---

*Farmers, fishermen and traders would gather in the market square to sell their wares every fifth day, which was known as Market Day.

trench we had dug near the chicken pen. My father and my cousin, Jose Cordeiro, were at the Public Works Department (PWD) Office which was just a stone's throw away from our house. They saw a bomb falling in the area of our house and came running back to see how we were. It was a direct hit on our house!

'When we came out from the trench we were shocked to see the front part of our house totally damaged. No one would have survived if they had been inside. That night, we slept in the space under the house, which was built on wooden pillars with the floor a few feet above the ground.

'Many people died in that first bombing of Taunggyi. Fortunately, there was no ground combat as the British retreated just before the Japanese troops entered. The British arranged trucks for anyone who wanted to evacuate the place, especially those who wanted to leave for India. So, six days after the bombing, we packed a few things, got on a truck and travelled north more than 300 miles to Hsipaw and from there by train to Mandalay and Mogaung in Central Burma. We were heading for the last remaining airport in Myitkyina, where some Allied planes were carrying people to India.

'While we were in Mogaung, word came to us that the Japanese had captured Myitkyina airport and a plane full of refugees had been bombed just as they were taking off. Now there was no way out of Burma by air or by sea. Many people decided to start walking, ready to take the dangerous route through thick jungle and high mountains. We were stranded in Mogaung as my brother, Alexius, who was a victim of polio, could not attempt the walk; besides, my mother was not really strong enough. So, we all decided to try and make our way back to Taunggyi.

'It wasn't easy to do that either, because of roadblocks and lack of transport. We first went to Samao and lived there for about a month. Then the Japanese authorities took us to Naba, a malarial place. Many people, especially the old, lost their lives to malaria and every day we would help bury the dead. At first we used to dig the graves at least five feet deep, but there were so many deaths that later we had no time or energy to dig more than three feet or so.

'We were fortunate to have survived, but perhaps Alexius and Joe picked up the disease there, because soon after we left Naba and went to Mandalay they became quite sick with malaria. We were given shelter at Don Bosco's Salesian house and Father Allessi treated them from his small supply of medicines. Alexander too contracted yellow fever and was often down with fever.

'We did not stay very long in Mandalay as we wanted to get back to familiar territory. So we made our way back to Taunggyi. As our house there was razed to the ground, we went to stay with our friends, the Naidu family, who offered us their hospitality. Later we moved to a small house in the Catholic Church compound. There in October 1942, Patrick, my nephew and the first of the new generation of Vazes, was born.

'When we were living under Japanese rule, we had to call them "masters". Although Japanese soldiers were everywhere, they didn't bother us much and we tried not to get in their way. Any fair-skinned person was suspected of having British ties and was arrested and put in camps. They even questioned my sister-in-law, Lucy*, but left us alone after that. There was a scarcity of food but fortunately my brother Robert, who worked in the Civil Supplies, could earn some money and sometimes he was also given rations like salt, sugar, and the like to bring home. So we were comparatively better off than many others, although we did go through a lot of hardship.

'Alexander, Joe and Jose too worked for the Garrison Engineer and earned some Japanese money. My father managed to buy a flour mill at Nagaba-Chaung village on the outskirts of Taunggyi, so we all went to live there for some time. I helped my father buy wheat, grind it with hydro power from the village stream and sell it for a small profit. Later I also worked for the Public Works Department in Loilem, some miles away from Taunggyi.

'Towards the end of 1944 and at the beginning of 1945 the British were pushing their way back into Burma, so there were some skirmishes between the Allied troops and the Japanese who were retreating. We had to be careful not to get in between the two armies. The Allied planes dropped supplies, and sometimes men, by parachutes. The Japanese were now on the defensive. They had previously trained a group of local young men—including many of our friends— to be interpreters after teaching them the Japanese language. Now the British were gaining ground and these interpreters knew too many secrets of the Japanese. So they were taken out of Taunggyi and shot dead. This came as a great shock to us amidst our optimism that we would be liberated from Japanese rule soon.

---

*See Introduction for an account of this.

'Only when the British returned victorious were we able to rebuild our house on the main road of Taunggyi. Even then all we could afford or get was bamboo- or wood-and-mat walls. After almost four years of turmoil and insecurity, we went back to the way things were before the war. My father, and my brothers, Alexander, Joe and Jose, got back their jobs in the PWD. Anthony and I went back to Insein and completed our studies. Later, Robert joined medical college and Frank attended the agricultural college. We continued living in Burma till we came back to Goa in 1966.

'Sometimes I wonder what way our lives would have gone if we had managed to escape to India in 1942. But we are grateful that all of us survived the war in Burma despite the hardships, while many others lost their lives trekking across the border to India.'

*

The late Gerald D'Souza gives us interesting insights into how his family lived under Japanese rule in a village near Maymyo and Mandalay. His father's music charmed the Japanese soldiers and kept them safe during the Japanese occupation.

'Not wishing to join the exodus, Grandfather Alex took his daughter Margaret, his wife Mary, along with her sisters, Maud, Kate and Agatha (who had remained spinsters, probably to keep between themselves the wealth of their parents) to Kalaw. Michael, his son, joined them soon after. This hill-station would escape unscathed during the war, being out of the direct path of the advancing Japanese forces.

'My father, Martin, had not considered it practical to join the gruelling exodus to Manipur with such small children, (Anne was then five, Gerald was three, and Benedict, born in March 1941, just a year old.) Nor could they have joined their relatives in Kalaw, as all access to it from Maymyo had been blocked by this time. Instead, he shifted the family to one of the Gurkha-dominated villages called Mogyibin, on the outskirts of Maymyo, even as the Japanese 18th Division, commanded by Lt. General Renya Mutaguchi, entered the Maymyo hill-station on May 8, 1942, and made the former British Governor's mansion his headquarters. Soon, a few other Goans similarly stranded in Upper Burma, including Nascimento Rodrigues, also came to reside in the vicinity of Mogyibin. Here they all constructed bashas (Burmese thatched bamboo huts built on stilts) for themselves, and here they survived for the next three years. They did so largely by growing their own maize and utilising whatever savings they had hoarded in the form of gold ornaments or King George V sovereigns and silver rupees, to buy local produce, vegetables, dairy products and other essentials. Paper currency, both British, as well as the new Japanese issue, the latter beautifully printed in red and green but without promise of redemption, had very little value at this time, resulting in uncontrollable inflation. Barter trade became more common.

'Of all the Japanese-occupied countries, Burma suffered worst during the invasion. Many of her towns had been reduced to ashes by air-raids. Her oil-wells, mining equipment, and river transport—including the steamers of the great Irrawady Flotilla Company—were deliberately destroyed in the "scorched earth" policy of the retreating British so as to be useless to the enemy. Allied air-raids from India continued to keep the railways out of action.

'All of Burma's normal external markets were also lost. The complete stoppage of her rice export led to mere subsistence farming. The south suffered from a glut of rice, while the north starved. The inability to import urgently needed consumer goods caused the greatest distress. Lower Burma was almost completely deprived of cooking oil, which only the dry zone of Central Burma could supply. The peasantry lost a large proportion of their indispensable cattle through the combination of military requisitions for food and a disease epidemic.

'Malaria control measures ceased and the people suffered heavily from the disease, including from a deadlier *Formosa* strain that had accompanied the invaders. There were epidemics of smallpox, cholera and bubonic plague, against which the authorities had to take drastic preventive measures.

'In December 1942, the British brigadier, Orde Wingate, with his special training force named the Chindits, marched across from Imphal to Tonhe on the Chindwin River to carry out a campaign of sabotage and destruction on the Mandalay–Myitkyina railway. The Chindits prowled murderously beyond the railway for several weeks, even sending a small contingent on an unsuccessful attempt to bring down the great Gohteik viaduct on the road and railway between Maymyo and Lashio, before they were forced to withdraw. For weeks thereafter, the Japanese Kempetai (military police) scoured the route of the Chindits' advance to round up any men that may have been left behind, either involuntarily or deliberately for clandestine operations.

'In the course of this search, one Captain Tanaka visited

Mogyibin to check on the antecedents of any non-native persons living there. During this process, he visited the basha where Martin and his family were residing. Seeing a piano in a village like this made the officer wonder whether it concealed a wireless transmitter or receiver. He asked for it to be stripped down to bare components. Martin not only did this, but demonstrated its true nature by playing a sad Japanese tune, "Sado Okesa", from a songbook he had once purchased out of curiosity at a festival of Japanese art and culture organised by the Japan–Burma Friendship Association at Mandalay in 1940, when British–Japanese relations had been relatively cordial. Martin went on to play all of the tunes in the book to the delight of the officer and his companions. He then explained to them that his family hailed from Goa, a colony of the Portuguese, who were neutral in the war.

'Thereafter, Captain Tanaka would occasionally call at the basha with members of his troop in the course of their patrols, bringing sweets or a bottle of sake (Japanese rice wine) or sometimes packets of quinine tablets, since there was an epidemic of malaria in the area, and once, even a Japanese doll for my new sister, Theresa, who had been born in July 1943. They would stay on to listen to Japanese songs, with sad and nostalgic expressions, rather than the stern expressions they usually had. They even taught me to sing a catchy Japanese military march—Ima koso-u teto senso ono—which I still remember.

'In time, Martin was given a paid assignment to play these songs and others which the Japanese would hum and he would note down, twice a week at the old Candacraig Hotel. This hotel had by then been taken over and converted into a rest and recreation centre for Japanese convalescing officers, generally after treatment at the Civil Hospital in Maymyo, which was now manned by Japanese military doctors. To facilitate his movement, Martin was given a new bicycle and, more importantly, an ivory seal with his name and occupation embossed in Japanese script, which he used to pass through the several security check posts along the way to Maymyo.

'By mid-1943, in the face of growing threats from the Allied forces who were poised to reconquer Burma, the Japanese had begun to lose their usual confidence. They decided that everything must be done to win over the peoples of the occupied countries and enlist them to resist Allied attacks. Their method was to set up puppet regimes with the semblance of independence.

'On August 1, 1943, the Japanese declared Burma an independent nation under the presidency of Dr Ba Maw, who took the title of "Adipadi". In Burmese, the title of naing-ngan-daw-adipadi is literally translated into "paramount ruler of the State". Thakin Aung San became Minister of Defence, his brother-in-law Than Tun, Minister of Transport and Supply, Brigadier Ne Win was made Commander of the Burmese National Army and Thakin Nu became Foreign Minister.

'The Karenni State and most of the Shan State were included as part of this new nation. There was no talk of reviving the Constitution of 1937 and, in any case, real control was in the hands of Dr Gotara Ogawa, formerly a cabinet minister in Tokyo, who became the "Supreme Advisor" to the Burmese government. Present at the independence ceremony was the Indian leader, Subhas Chandra Bose. Previously in Singapore, Bose had taken command of the 40,000 odd Indian prisoners-of-war, formerly in British service, who were captured by the Japanese. He had formed the Indian National Army (INA), under the auspices of the Indian Independence League dedicated to evicting the British from India in concert with the Japanese. Bose held meetings in Maymyo telling the audience about the Indian struggle for independence.

'Martin learnt about the political developments going on in the rest of Burma from *Greater Asia*, an English-language newspaper published in Singapore and circulated in Burma. The issue dated January 7, 1944, had on its cover a photograph of a slim and elegant Burmese lady shaking hands with an Indian one, dressed in a rumpled military uniform. The caption read "The First Lady of Burma, H.E. Daw Khin Ma Maw and the First Lady of the Azad Hind Dal, Dr S. Lakshmi". The Burmese lady was, of course, the wife of Dr Ba Maw, Head of State. Dr S. Lakshmi had been a paediatrician in Singapore who volunteered to join and ultimately head the INA's small Rani of Jhansi women's regiment.

'One day, Captain Tanaka informed Martin at the Candacraig Hotel that the officers of the Indian Independence League wished to stage a variety entertainment programme on March 30, 1944 for men about to leave for the front. They were to join Yamamoto's Regiment at Tamu to be present at the fall of Imphal and to line the route at Bose's triumphant entry into Manipur. It was to be an open-air show and Martin was requested to accompany the singers on the piano in performing some patriotic Indian songs.

They would all be singing in unison, hence Martin could improvise his own introduction and accompaniment. Accordingly, one of the singers came forward and, by listening to him, Martin made his notations for the selected songs.

'The programme began with humorous satires on the desperate situation of the British Indian Army, while BBC ("Bluff & Bluster Corporation") bulletins were parodied, with clipped British accents: "The Japanese have retained the initiative in their advance through Manipur and INA troops are advancing up the Kaladan; they have also occupied Paletwa, Tiddim and Tongzang. Falam and Fort White have fallen into the enemy's hands. Our 17th Division is in full retreat. The Imphal–Silchar Road has been cut. The situation is serious but not critical." The audience laughed uproariously.

'When it came to the patriotic songs, however, it turned out that the singers, among them Prem Sahgal, the military secretary, had more enthusiasm than musical talent. They all started singing in different keys! Martin bravely played on through the ensuing cacophony. Eventually, he had his photograph taken in the company of Bose, Prem Sahgal and Dr A.C. Chatterjee. He would preserve this photo long after the event.

Just as the programme concluded, when the the audience had dispersed and the soldiers gone off to their camp, the moon came up—and so did the Allied bombers. One bomb struck very close to where the girls of the Rani of Jhansi Regiment had been staying, blocking their entrance. When the debris was cleared away and the girls crept out of the air-raid shelters, they saw their building had been reduced to matchwood. No one was hurt, but they had lost their rifles and all their clothing, except what they stood up in. They were then shifted to another empty house, one of several in Maymyo that had formerly been owned by Indian expatriates, and had been possessed by the Indian Independence League (IIL) based on an understanding with the Japanese. Khaki cloth being in short supply, they were given regular uniforms meant for men, and a sewing machine with which to alter them.

'During the next two years, dramatic events began unfolding. The Japanese had been confident of victory in Imphal and Kohima on the Indian side of the border, but they suffered heavy losses and were forced to retreat. After American forces (Merrill's Marauders) captured Myitkyina airport in Northern Burma and General Stilwell's army recaptured the China Road, the Japanese started retreating from the north. By January 1945, the whole of the northern area was cleared of Japanese soldiers. The liberated areas of Upper Burma were thereafter brought under the Civil Affairs Service (Burma), known as the CAS(B). The CAS(B) had been tasked with re-establishing civil order, restoring the administration of the towns and villages, restoring basic civic and medical services, indenting and rationing scarce foodstuffs and undertaking other such assignments to bring the area under their care to some semblance of pre-war normalcy. Under it were welfare officers—mostly drawn from former British government servants, still in the country—who were to interact with the common people and ensure that these benefits reached them.

'Martin applied for the post of welfare officer, got selected and was accommodated with his family in one of the empty houses in the elite southeast quarter of the town. The old rented house they had lived in before the war had been one of the casualties of a stray British bomb. Nearby, the church had remained unscathed, though unpainted and covered with moss. As the residents and the clergy, including Fr. Moindrot, began to trickle back in, Martin resumed playing the pipe-organ for Sunday services.

'As someone very familiar with the topography of the Northern Shan State, in his role as welfare officer, Martin was especially assigned the task of communicating with former residents of Maymyo, who—like himself—had taken refuge in various villages in the Northern Shan State, as well as the hundreds of European or Eurasian prisoners of war. The latter had been held by the Japanese in camps just beyond Mongyo along the China–Burma Road, at Mangshih, Lungling, Huangsakan and Shankiakai, then released just before their guards had retreated south through Hsipaw into the Shan hills. Martin's task was to bring all the refugees and prisoners of war to Mongyo, accommodate them temporarily in the hundreds of bamboo-and-thatch bashas erected there, and register them for rations and other civil supplies. Then, he had to send them to Assam by military transport over the Stilwell Road, if they so desired, and if not, bring them to Maymyo. Here, they were to be accommodated in the hundreds of houses left vacant in the exodus of 1942, or in wooden cantonments built on open grounds. For this work, he was provided with two deuce-and-a-half tonne military trucks and the requisite complement of drivers, cleaners and armed security guards, all Gurkhas.

'Martin was also able to visit Kalaw via Hsipaw to assure himself of the well-being of the rest of the family, including

Maud, Kate, and Agatha. They had, in the meanwhile, adopted two little Burmese orphans, named Colette and Esther. He returned to Maymyo with Alex and Margaret in time to celebrate Easter jointly with the Rodrigues family. They also enjoyed Thingyan, the water festival marking the Burmese New Year, with the entire local community. Their plans included a picnic to the Anisakan waterfalls on the outskirts of the town.

'Meanwhile, the main Japanese Army was so heavily defeated at Meiktila, that it began to disintegrate. As Dr Ba Maw, who also retreated with the Japanese, would later write in his memoirs*: "Two armies, Japanese and Indian, and two governments, Burmese and Indian, and an endless throng of vehicles in all sorts of conditions moving at all sorts of speed choked the whole length of the narrow road to Pegu and everything was just crawling along and even brought at times to a long halt, while the brilliant moon shone pitilessly showing up every object on this road."

'The refugees, for that was what they had become, were vulnerable to British air attack as they moved along in decrepit old buses or on foot. The Japanese refused to provide the members of the Burmese government with military transport. From the very first night of the retreat, April 23, 1945 bombing and strafing of the slow column was continuous.

'Ba Maw was worried by personal events as much as by international ones. His eldest daughter, Tinsa, was about to

---

*Maw, Ba. *Breakthrough in Burma: 1939-46.* Yale University Press, New Haven. 1968

have her first child, who was in fact born at Kyaikto on the night of April 28th, after she had been driven nearly out of her mind by the rigours of the journey and the constant bombing and machine-gunning from the air.

'The Arzi Hukumat-e-Hind under Subhas Chandra Bose was also part of the same retreat, but with the signal difference that Bose himself had refused motor transport at one stage of the journey and had insisted on sharing the hardships of the march with his men. He had in fact wanted to stay on in Rangoon till the end, but his ministers had persuaded him to make for Bangkok. He had thirty-nine women under his command, too, which added to his responsibilities. Their commander, Dr S. Lakshmi, had been trapped behind enemy lines, while on a visit to Kalaw to set up a hospital there. She was later taken prisoner and repatriated to India.

Incidentally, most of the INA troops had already surrendered by this time, some in the Irrawaddy valley (near Mount Popa) and others at Zeywadi. Nevertheless, Subhas Chandra Bose seems to have had more concern for Burma's capital than the Premier, Ba Maw, himself. Rangoon had suffered terribly from British bombing in the spring of 1945. The railway station had been wiped out and big buildings in the centre were just so many shells. Bombing had destroyed the water supply; there had been no water in Rangoon since March 22, 1945, and this had the ancillary effect of causing the sewage system to break down. The generating station had been bombed, there was no electricity, and transport by road was extremely hazardous. In the port, 60 per cent of the wharfage and 80 per cent of the covered accommodation had been destroyed. There was no doubt Rangoon would be vulnerable to looting and pillage on a grand scale once the Japanese had left, and since Bose felt a grave responsibility towards the remaining Indian population of the city, he had instructed Major-General A.D. Loganathan to stay behind in command of 5,000 troops of the INA, to maintain order in Rangoon until the British arrived and began their new administration.

'On May 1, 1945, the British 17th Indian Division reached Pegu and, on the following day, the outskirts of Rangoon. The advance had been so swift that the plan for a sea-borne assault on Rangoon—which also took place—was rendered almost superfluous. The British tactically let Aung San's army enter the devastated city first. All along, Major General Pearce and the senior officers of the Civil Affairs Service had not liked the idea of making use of the Burma Independence Army, but had been overruled by Lord Mountbatten. Shortly after the capture of Rangoon, Pearce again pressed for Aung San to be arrested and tried as a traitor. Mountbatten rejected this advice and, soon after, replaced Pearce by Major General Sir Hubert Rance as head of the CAS(B).

'Meanwhile, Martin continued working as Welfare Officer, to receive and rehabilitate in Maymyo other refugees, who had fled into interiors so deep that even after the war had ended with the surrender of Japan in August 1945, they were not aware of it.

'In February 1946, my twin-brothers, Fintan Ignatius and Colman Francis, were born and baptised on March 2nd of that year, in the Church of the Immaculate Conception by Fr. Moindrot.

'Sir Hubert Rance visited Maymyo, took stock of the rehabilitation work being done and reassigned some of the officers to other liberated parts of Burma. In the course of this, Martin was designated Welfare Officer for Amherst

District, and reassigned to the Tennessarim coast, in the southernmost part of Burma where there were numerous camps between Thanbyuzayat and the Three-Pagoda pass bordering Siam (present-day Thailand), still holding former prisoners-of-war, who had been used to build the railway on this route (later made famous by the movie *Bridge on the River Kwai*). He shifted his family from Maymyo to Moulmein, where my youngest brother, Anthony, was born.'

His son, Gerald, concludes: 'Martin took me from Moulmein to Rangoon, where I met for the first time grandmother Mary and uncle Michael, my three grand-aunts and adopted cousins. The family coordinated plans to repatriate to Goa as had been decided. The grand-aunts were the first to sail. They were already settled in a house at St. Inez, Panjim by the time the rest of the family reached Goa in the summer of 1948, excluding Michael who had decided to remain in Rangoon. Michael had returned to his business as a partner in the pharmaceutical company of E.M. D'Souza but a few years later he too joined us.'

*

Kevin Pinto and his mother, Cecelia Pinto, who came from the large Machado clan (established by Francis, Michael and Santan Machado, three brothers from Saligao who migrated to Burma in the early 1900s) left Burma for India by boat. He narrates how his uncle and his father, Tertulian Pinto, who was a guard in the Burma Railways, attempted to trek across the border but turned back to help some nuns: 'By the time Uncle Fred and my dad were free to leave for India, the sea routes were closed and the only way out was to trek to India. They managed to get to Myitkyina, in the north of Burma. From here they made their way west and arrived at a staging post. I cannot remember the name of this town. Here they hoped to join a group for the trek to India. They noticed a group of Catholic nuns and a lot of young children. Uncle Fred asked one of the nuns what they were doing there in the middle of nowhere. She said they were taking the orphans to India. Dad and Uncle Fred managed to talk them out of it by convincing them that the safest place for them was Rangoon. This was reasoned on the premise that as the nuns were all Irish, of the Good Shepherd Order, and Ireland was neutral in the war, the Japanese would not molest or harm them in any way. To ensure their safety, Dad and Uncle Fred accompanied them back to Rangoon and offered all the help that they could give them. They managed to find some housing but it was a very difficult existence as by now, Rangoon was under Japanese occupation.

'One day, Uncle Fred saw some Japanese soldiers marching and recognised their commander. I do not know his name or rank so for the purposes of this narrative, I will refer to him as the General. Uncle Fred told the Sisters that the General was a former pupil of his when he was a lecturer at Rangoon University and he would try to get his help. He went to the Japanese Headquarters to try and meet with the General and there he was subjected to much verbal and physical abuse, but he persisted in his request for an interview and was successful. The soldiers allowed him into the General's presence, perhaps to see him further humiliated. When the two met it was the General who bowed to Uncle Fred and asked: "Saya*, what can I do for you?"

---

*Saya is a respectful term which the Burmese people use to address male teachers. Female teachers are called Sayama.

'Uncle Fred came straight to the point and said, "You have taken all the convents that the nuns own and now they have nowhere to house the orphans and take proper care of them."

'The General agreed to let them have one convent and that was the one on Prome Road.

'The sisters now had good accommodation. Food was still a problem. So Uncle Fred decided to try his luck once more. He went back to the General. This time he was led straight to his office. "Saya, what can I do for you now?" asked the General.

"You have given them accommodation but they have no food. Can you do something about it?" The General decided to give them food and for the duration of the Japanese occupation they were supplied with enough food for the sisters and the orphans.

'But Uncle Fred was not satisfied. He returned to the General and complained that the Japanese were occupying two other convents and not paying rent. The General had a little smile on his face. He agreed to pay rent and said that was all he could do for them. The attitude of the General speaks well for the respect that students and former students in Asia accord their teachers. It cuts right through racial and enemy lines.

'One of the sisters was an excellent seamstress and dressmaker. The Japanese heard of this and wanted her to sew some clothes for their wives. My dad, a very bashful man, was given the task of measuring them for the fittings. He was most embarrassed at having to do this but managed, even with his eyes almost closed. The money earned for this work helped to augment their income.

'Some time in 1943, a British plane was shot down over Rangoon. The pilot parachuted and landed somewhere in the convent grounds. The Japanese were there in a few minutes. They searched everywhere but could not find the airman. When they left, the nuns heard some sounds coming out of their well. The airman had landed in the well and had broken both his legs. One of the sisters went down the well, put him on her shoulders and brought him up. He was hidden successfully in the convent for the duration of the war. To get rid of the evidence, the parachute was cut up into six-inch squares and sewn into handkerchiefs. The Pinto family got four of these, embroidered with our initials, one each for my mom, sister, brother and me. The Japanese paper money had no real monetary value, so before the war ended Uncle Fred used the money earned in rent and dressmaking to make repairs to the convent.'

Chapter 9

Refugees in India

Evacuees from Burma who reached India were given some assistance by the British government. Many of them had relatives and homes to go to in India, but even those who didn't, managed to establish themselves in places like Belgaum. Camps were established in Chunar, near Allahabad, and at some other places where the refugee families were looked after.

'A.J. D'Cruz and family, including Donald and Thelma Menezes, as well as Isabelle Vaz and Felicity Fernandes, all tell of being given shelter, food and medicines in makeshift camps on the grounds of Loretto Convent as soon as they arrived in Calcutta. From there, they were given monetary aid and train tickets for their onward journey. Doris D'Mello and Lena Rego were given similar aid when their families landed in Madras. Doris remembers that they were given clothes, food and money and also tickets to travel to Goa by train. Even while they stayed at the maternal family home in Saligao, she remembers getting books and pencils, besides food. Later, her father worked in the Army and Navy Store in Bombay. In December 1947 they returned to Burma.

Lena Rego recalls being taken care of in Madras and later travelling to their maternal grandmother's house in Saligao, Goa. 'We stayed in Goa for five months and I am truly grateful to my grandmother and aunt who took care of our big family and showed us such kindness. My grandmother suggested that we establish ourselves in Belgaum instead of Goa, because the cost of living was cheap there and there were good schools where we could continue with our education. So we settled in Belgaum. Our joy was complete when my brother Lucas was reunited with us.'

*

Donald Menezes narrates what took place soon after their arrival in Calcutta. 'We were taken to the refugee camp at Loretto Convent by buses and given hot tea and buns by the good nuns. The next morning, our old Burma friends, the O'Learys, found us there and took us to their Calcutta home. They were very kind, paying most attention to Grandpa, who was close to a breakdown. Arnold was burning with fever so I took him to the hospital. A blood test showed malaria. I was feverish too, and my blood test also confirmed malaria. But the hospital was overfull. So I was given quinine pills and sent home. My sister had now recovered. So we took the train to Nagpur. No one was at the station to greet us. But we found our way home to a joyous reunion. Later, there was a great family reunion, as our cousins from Bombay came to greet and lionise the returned "Burma Refugees".'

*

Donald's grandpa, A.J. D'Cruz, gives his touching version of their first few days after getting to India: 'After a night's sleep in the camp, I got up at 5 a.m. and went to look for Mrs Furtado's house in McLeod Street. I met an old lady walking out of the lane and I asked her where the Furtados were living. She said, "Don't trouble me. You look for them yourself." The house was a big mansion, a four-storeyed building known as King's Chambers. There was no signboard so I could not find it. I boarded a tramcar and though lots of people got in, no one would sit next to me. Of course, I looked like a beggar as I had been wearing the same clothes for the past twenty-five days from Mawlaik to Calcutta. During the journey, I had walked in heavy rains and floods and also slept in the same clothes. I told the passengers that I was not a beggar but a Burma evacuee and had just arrived after trekking for twenty-five days. They simply smiled and I thought they were probably afraid that I might ask for help so they left me alone.

'The car arrived at Esplanade in due time and I got out and went in search of Captain O'Leary. I went up by lift to his flat on the fourth floor and when his eldest daughter opened the door and saw me she shouted, "Mr D'Cruz!" The whole family came out and gave me a warm welcome and served me tea and cake inside. I then learnt that my daughter, Emily, and grandson, Donald, were with them, but my son, Arnold, was in hospital with malaria. Captain O'Leary brought my children and our luggage from the camp and we stayed there for five days.

'After arriving in Calcutta, I started showing signs of malaria; this continued for five days. Then Mrs Furtado took us to her house and I was treated at her place by Dr Braganza Cunha. Mrs Furtado nursed me back to health.

'While in Calcutta I came to know that my daughter Sophie had arrived from Akyab with her husband and children and had proceeded to Nagpur, leaving a note for me. I wired her of our arrival and she wired back, asking us all to come to Nagpur. We reached Nagpur on May 15, 1942. Our passage all along was paid by the government, including the travelling expenses of all members of my family and the servant. Even after our arrival here, the Women's Voluntary Services ladies committee showed us so much hospitality and kindness and visited us frequently, bringing gifts for the young people. I must mention here that Mrs Registrar has been exceptionally kind to all evacuees in Nagpur. May God bless her and all members of the committee.'

*

Thelma Menezes tells that hundreds of refugees died of cerebral malaria, many while trekking, and others in the 'Burma Ward' specially set up in the Howrah General Hospital in Calcutta. She relates the events that took place when her family landed in Calcutta and thereafter: 'My in-laws and my family came in safe, but my husband arrived in Calcutta splattered with blood. Sharpnel had entered his thigh during the bombing of Imphal. He was moved to Bombay for an operation. In Bombay we stayed with Dr Fernand Rodrigues, a retired Civil Surgeon originally from Saligao who had left Burma by boat just before the Japanese invasion. Finally we landed in Belgaum to be reunited with the Machados and San Lazaros. Bonded by the trek out of Burma, we began to start a new life.

'Financially, there was no problem as the British government had directed that refugees would be paid their pensions, salaries and savings through an office in Simla. My father took up the post of Public Prosecutor in Bhalgapur. My mother joined the Howrah General Hospital as Matron.

After his education in Calcutta, my brother went back and was commissioned in the Burmese army. My sister, a doctor, also went back as Medical Officer of the Burma Oil Company. My younger brother, an engineer, opted for India. My husband got a commission in the British army and went back to Burma with the Allied troops. Later, he was absorbed into the Indian army.'

*

Felicity Fernandes' family too was given shelter in a makeshift camp put up by the government in the grounds of Loretto House. After a day or two, they were all transported to their various destinations. She says, 'Bridget recalls Mum telling her that during our short stay there, the Irish sisters would very kindly come and carry her (then just a child of about two) off to their community room to play with her. By a unique coincidence, seventeen years later, she joined the same congregation in Kolkata! She and I, my daughters and Ed's daughters, owe our education to this beloved Irish Loretto Institute, to whom we will always be indebted for the values and principles ingrained in us.

'Once we arrived in Goa from Kolkata, Mum was able to relax as her beloved mother and only brother, Efante Cardoso, took over the care of us all. We were enrolled in school without delay and relaxed in the warmth and love of her family, relatives and neighbours. If Mum was worried, she never did let us know, but she was anxious about Dad of whom there was no news at all. We were all so relieved and happy when Dad managed to survive the trek and arrived to be reunited with us.'

*

Albert deSouza recollects that on their arrival in Calcutta, the British gave them a warm welcome. They were given shelter in St. Xavier's College and stayed there for some days till the Jesuit priests helped them to get train tickets to Goa. They first went to Albert's maternal family home in Tivim and later also stayed at their father's village of Nadora. Later, they moved to other parts of India.

*

Patricia Duarte who came with her parents and her maternal aunt's family writes, 'The boat arrived in Madras and there we went our separate ways. We went on by train to Bombay to stay at Aunt Cassie's (Casilda Duarte) place and the others went by train to Calcutta where our many Jewish relatives lived. This was the last time that we would ever see them and the last time for me to see my Jewish family (besides my mum and her brother who visited us twice).

'I didn't like Bombay at all and missed Rangoon. I remember how crowded and completely different Bombay was. I loved Rangoon. It was the capital of Burma but it was spacious and not at all like Bombay which was noisy and bustling, while Rangoon was serene. There were many nice trees and large parks,' she remembers.

*

Leo Rego says, 'When we got to Calcutta, we were given shelter in the Loretto Convent but we could not stay there for more than a few days because it was packed with refugees from Burma, with more coming in daily. Luckily we got tickets to travel to Goa by train, and after the long journey we arrived at my dad's family home in Assagao in North

Goa. In Goa then, there were no electric street lights and it was pitch dark as we felt our way up to the house. My father's sister who was staying in the house burst into tears when she saw us at the door. She had had no news of us and was worrying about our safety. She was so relieved as she took us in and cared for us and we too felt safe at last.

'Dad's wish was that we should continue our schooling and the closest "good" school he found out was at Arpora, a few miles away from our home. So he rented a house in Arpora and we boys attended St. Joseph's High School.

Like a miracle, on August 15th, the Feast of the Assumption of Our Lady, when we had just returned from church after evening service, George and John appeared at our door in army uniforms. Needless to say we were all overjoyed and found it incredible that they had found their way from Burma to Arpora in search of the family. In the meantime, while in Arpora two of my brothers hurt themselves falling from a tree—one broke an ankle and the other hurt his knee—so my dad had to take them to Bombay for treatment. Here he heard about a camp for Burma refugees in Chunar near Allahabad. He decided that we would all go and live in Chunar. Although there was no electricity or running water, we were safe and comfortable in the camp. When the British and their Allies recaptured Burma in 1945 they took us all back to Rangoon by ship.'

*

Chunar was the location of an early settlement for European officials and was maintained by the British government. It had sports grounds, a small hospital and a small school. It was an ideal place for the British government to accommodate the Burmese refugees. A British lady was the camp commandant. The evacuees were given free housing and also some financial assistance.

Wilma Silgardo recalls, 'We landed on the shores of India on February 7th. Later we went to Ajra near Belgaum, where my priest uncle was, and stayed in the church premises. My parents and the others who had come to India by plane, joined us after some weeks.'

*

Tony Machado's parents too opted for Belgaum, because of its proximity to Goa which was under Portuguese rule. 'Belgaum was the best choice because of its good schools and colleges and low cost of living,' he explains. Tony is not aware of any aid from the British government and he says they had to start from scratch because all of his Dad's investments in Burma were lost.

Chapter 10

Return to Burma—A Historical Perspective

For more than two years the Japanese ruled as 'masters' in Burma, living out what they believed was God's divine plan for their superior race. They had shown that they could defeat the great Western powers. In the meantime, the British were planning operations to recapture Burma while based on the Indian side of the Indo–Burma border. Burma was strategically located between India and China. For the British, the defence of Burma was key to the defence of India, the 'crown jewel' in the British Empire. For the Japanese, destroying the Burma–China road and blocking US military aid to China was one of their main aims.

The first advances into Burma, carried out in 1942 and 1943, were a source of military frustration for the British. The Japanese grew formidable in defence as they had in attack. A second campaign was launched by the Chindits* under the leadership of Brigadier General Orde Wingate.

---

*Chindits were the mythological half-lion half-griffins, statues of which stand guard over Burmese pagodas to ward off evil spirits. The word is also used for lions, the kings of the jungle.

He had set up camps in India where he trained his men until they were hardened in jungle warfare. They entered northern Burma through Assam, using mules whose vocal chords had been cut. They forced their way through virgin jungle, attacked Japanese outposts, destroyed bridges, and ambushed and killed a number of Japanese soldiers there. But the Chindits suffered untold hardships. Hunger, dysentery, diarrhoea and malaria reduced the strong hearty men to near skeletons. The soldiers ate insects, rats, monkeys, and sucked out the fluids from green bamboos. One-third of them died, and the rest who were ordered to withdraw, returned to their base in Assam ravaged with disease. Some 600 of them never recovered to fight again.

Although the campaign failed, it proved that the British troops could fight on equal terms with the Japanese in the jungle using a combination of modern and primitive warfare. Local tribesmen, especially the Kachins, living in the hills of north-eastern Burma, cooperated with the Allies using guerilla tactics against the Japanese. They made booby traps in which they placed sharp bamboo sticks smeared with faeces. This not only impaled the Japanese and bled them to death, but infected the wounds with fatal results. The Kachins moved silently around the Japanese camps, stealthily killing and cutting off the ears of the dead men. This had a psychologically terrifying effect on the Japanese, who believe that human bodies must go to paradise whole and undefiled.

By 1944, the Japanese had advanced to Imphal and Kohima near the Indo–Burma border. They intended to seize British supplies in Assam and also to inspire Indians to rise against the British. But the Allies held out against the attack, and forced the enemy to withdraw down the

Chindwin River. The 14th Indian Army, a multinational force comprising British, Indians, West Africans and soldiers from other parts of Europe, pursued the Japanese and in the process suffered heavy casualties. The Chindits and Burma Rifles too suffered untold hardship and lost many men, but they succeeded in weakening the Japanese force in Burma. The monsoons, malaria and starvation also took their toll on the Japanese soldiers and their bodies littered the road.

It was now a concerted campaign. The tribesmen of Burma were equipped with weapons by the Allies and played an important role in fighting the occupiers. Aung San's Burma National Army, trained and armed by the Japanese, were now cooperating with the Allies. The RAF, which was by now highly experienced, carried out air commando raids and provided air cover for the Chindits and the American forces under the leadership of General Stilwell. Chinese divisions too attacked the Japanese. This combined military campaign defeated the Japanese Army. The last great battle was fought in Mandalay, which fell in March 1945, and by May that year, the Allies recaptured Rangoon.

The Burma Campaign (1942–45), which was one of the longest and one of the most difficult campaigns in the Second World War, ended in victory for the Allies and the Burmese. It had been fought against a determined enemy over difficult and dangerous terrain by troops a long way from home. About 150,000 Japanese soldiers died in Burma, more than half the number who had come there.

The Burmese people welcomed the British as liberators, not as conquerors. What they really wanted was independence from foreign rule. The British took over the task of reconstructing the war-ravaged economy of the country.

*

Some of the Goan survivors went back to Burma to see if they could re-establish their lives in the old familiar surroundings.

Felicity Fernandes relates, 'Dad told us later that soon after we left Kalaw, he closed up the shop and left the keys with good Burmese friends in the hope that one day he could return. He did go back after the war but there was just a heap of rubble where once the building stood. He returned to India and the family soon after.'

*

Doris D'Mello's family too returned to Thaton, a town in Mon State in southern Burma. She said, 'It was really sad to see all the shops razed to the ground. Everything, even our homes, had disappeared. All that was left was rubble. But would you believe it? Our dog came running out from somewhere and jumped on my mother, and then greeted all of us. We left Thaton and went to live with some cousins in Rangoon. The airport was being rebuilt and my father got a job there as time-keeper. We continued our studies in Rangoon. I later trained as a nurse and worked in the Dufferin Hospital. The others got jobs in offices in Rangoon too.'

Doris worked as a nurse in Rangoon Dufferin Hospital till 1952. Her family left Burma for good then and gradually established themselves in India where she worked as a nurse in Bombay and later in Kuwait.

*

Sylvia D'Gama's brother, Willie Saldanha returned to Burma, married a Burmese lady, raised children and lived there till he died.

*

A great part of Isabelle Vaz's life was spent in Burma, before the war and after. She attended school at Branch Convent, while her brother Aloysious studied in St. Paul's High School. When they returned to Burma after the war, they continued their studies in the same schools. Later, when the Karen uprising occurred in 1949 they left the country again to settle in Mumbai.

'Destiny willed that I go back to Burma in 1957,' muses Isabelle. 'Frank Vaz, the youngest of the seven Vaz brothers who were living in the Shan State of Burma, came with his parents to India to find a bride. My parents knew the family well and felt that he was the perfect match for me. So we were married in Bombay, and left soon after for my new home in Taunggyi and later to Lashio.

'Since Frank was an agricultural officer, we lived in comfortable government quarters and enjoyed a life of plenty. After the military regime took over the reins of government, we decided to return to Goa in 1966. Frank passed away in Goa in 1999.

'Five of my six children were born in Burma and they were still young when we came away. So, initially, it was a bit of a struggle to begin a new life here. But Goa is home now, with sons-in-law, daughters-in-law and nine grandchildren added to the family and living in different parts of India and abroad. My heart is filled with love and gratitude for all blessings we have received,' concludes Isabelle.

*

Leo Rego and his whole family was taken back to Burma by ship in 1945. The British kept them in a camp in Kamayut and later at Branch Convent. 'My dad started looking around for a place of his own and since there were many houses being sold cheap, he managed to buy a house on 41st Street. My younger brothers and I went back to school at St. Paul's Catholic High School, and my elder brothers started working in Rangoon. My dad earned his living by teaching music as well as being an organist and choir master at St. Mary's Cathedral in Rangoon. One of my brothers joined the Salesian order in Maymyo but had to leave because his sight and hearing got affected when the school was bombed during the Karen uprising which took place soon after Burma got independence.

'My parents were very religious and very much involved in parish work. As Dad was the choir master in the Cathedral, we sometimes had to attend three masses on a Sunday as he needed us to sing in his choir. This upbringing has kept us close to the Catholic Church and my brothers and I are still involved in a lot of church activities, even after migrating to Australia following the death of our parents in Burma. The good values and the discipline that my parents have handed down to us live on in our family,' Leo remembers with gratitude.

*

Renee Pinto's father decided to go back to Burma with whatever little savings he had. He went back to Rangoon in 1946 and began working in the NAAFI (Navy, Army and Air Force Institutes), an organisation created by the British government in 1921 to run recreational establishments needed by the Armed Forces, and to sell goods to servicemen and their families. 'My mother, my elder brother Angelo and I too went to Rangoon in 1947,' says Renee. 'My brother's godfather, an Italian (whom I remember only as Mr Angelo), had his own business in Maymyo and it was he who persuaded my father to move back to Maymyo. So we all returned to Maymyo and with his savings plus help from Mr Angelo, he started a chemist shop of his own. It was the only chemist shop in Maymyo. My father had to work very hard in the beginning, but gradually business picked up. By the time my youngest brother, Ronnie, was born, in 1953, it had become a thriving business.

I have two other sisters, Hazel and Melba, who were born soon after we went back to Maymyo. My father sent Angelo and my two sisters all the way to Darjeeling, India, for their education. Angelo later joined the Medical College in Goa and became a doctor. We had a good life in Burma till 1965, when the military government nationalised our business. My father lost everything. No compensation was given so we came back to India like refugees for the second time.'

*

Especiosa D'Souza's husband Gilbert, who had joined the army, was transferred to Rangoon. 'We joined him in June 1947. When we arrived in Rangoon, Gilbert's brother Vincent was there to take us to our flat on 43rd Street, which had been cleaned and painted by Gilbert's sister's son-in-law. The rest of the family was in Bombay and Goa. Vincent travelled from Mergui (where he had his book agency) to Rangoon often to visit us. His wife, a Burmese lady, was killed in a car accident, when the vehicle they were travelling in was hit. He loved her so much that he kept her clothes with him till he died,' she reminisces.

'We loved Rangoon, and after Gilbert did his time in the army he worked for a small cycle agency and then for Crompton Engineering. We then had five more children—

Ronnie, Linda, Marlene, Arnold, who were all born in Rangoon, and Evelyn, who was born in Goa. They added to our Joe and Mirna.

'We had many Goan friends, the Silgardos, the Regos, the Fanas, the Newtons, the Saldanhas, Father Mascarenhas. We were parishioners of St. Mary's Cathedral and the parish priest was Father Fernandes, another Goan. The children went to Pastinas School (a private junior school) and then to St. John's Convent and the younger ones to Sacred Heart School which was attached to St. Mary's Church.

'Sundays was Mass, then spring cleaning the house, which was Gilbert's forte, while I cooked a picnic lunch and then all the kids were packed in the car and we would join friends at Inya Lake for a good swim or drive to the airport. Most evenings we went for a drive or for a snack or a glass of sugarcane juice. The market was close to us and we got the best fish and vegetables. (We still prepare a lot of Burmese food.) The hawkers with mohinga, kaukswe and other items were so clean, serving the meal from their baskets which they balanced on a stick.

'We had to leave Burma reluctantly to come back to Goa in June 1960 because we felt that the Burmans had changed towards foreigners, especially Indians and Chinese. We also had to come back to settle some property matters. Although there were times of difficulty and hardship, there are also fond memories of the good times we experienced in Burma, which I will always treasure.'

*

After the British recaptured Burma, Geraldine Pinto's father and her brother, Joseph, went back to Rangoon in 1946 and reopened Burma Café. But after three years, in 1949, they decided to close the business because the good quality ingredients which they needed were unavailable. So they returned to Goa.

*

Three of Wilma Silgardo's brothers went back to Burma when the British were declared victorious. They found the house standing undamaged, but there was nothing left inside. Everything had been stolen. Two of her brothers left Burma after some time, but Dr Olwen worked with the famous Dr Seagrave in the northern Shan State. When the military regime took over the reins of government in Burma, Dr Olwen was denied a visa to continue working in Burma. So he repatriated to Bangalore and lived there till he passed away.

*

In May 1945, when Rangoon was re-occupied, Hugh Nazareth immediately made efforts to get back into Burma. He left his wife and baby in Bombay. At this stage, only army personnel were being permitted entry into Burma. He went to Chittagong, where his friend Anju D'Souza was posted in the army, and pleaded for him to find some way for him to go to Burma. The Canteen Stores Department was sending shiploads of provisions to the troops and other personnel in Burma and they recruited local labour to load the goods onto the ship, travel on the ship and unload the goods at Rangoon Port. Anju got a khalasi's (dockyard worker's) uniform for Hugh, taught him how to march and salute, and got him into the gang of khalasis going on the next ship to Rangoon. While at sea, they were attacked by a Japanese submarine, in spite of being on a hospital ship painted white with a red cross. Fortunately, the torpedo went wide. Their ship promptly showed the white flag with the red cross. This was after August 6, 1945 when the first atomic bomb was dropped on Hiroshima and Japan had capitulated. The ship's captain signalled the submarine that the war was over. The commander of the Japanese submarine cautiously came to the surface and exchanged signals. When he was convinced, he came aboard and had some refreshments with the captain of the ship. He was apparently happy that the war was over and he could go home.

With no further incidents, the ship sailed up the Rangoon river and started unloading. As the khalasis were moving to and from the ship and the dock, Hugh found an opportunity to disappear in the dockside crowd. He then went to Toungoo to search for his Mum and sisters, from whom he had no news since the Japanese occupation of Burma.

On reaching Toungoo there was no sign of their house, just rubble. Hugh was not able to exactly locate where their house had stood. He asked an old rickshaw puller and he was surprised when this man was able to direct him to the site of their old home and also take him to where his family was living. Hugh was thus reunited with his Mum and sisters.

He rebuilt their house and restarted the business, initially as a British army contractor. When travel to and from Burma was open to the general public, he went back to Bombay and brought his wife and daughter to Toungoo. His next child, Hubert, was born at home with a midwife in attendance, as the hospital at Toungoo had not yet started functioning, though the building was complete.

As he was born and educated in Burma, Hugh knew many of the senior people in independent Burma's new government. Using all his old contacts, Hugh built up the business with his office in Phayre Street. He bought a house on 49th Street in Rangoon and shifted his wife and children there, while his Mum and sisters remained in Toungoo. His sister, Theresa, who had completed her B.A. and B.Ed. from Rangoon University was teaching at the local convent. His Mum died in Toungoo in 1945 and was buried next to his father in the Toungoo cemetery.

Hugh bought another house on the outskirts of Rangoon, but did not occupy it. An American gentleman approached him because he wanted to rent this house to live in. This American had established good contacts with the Chinese government of Generalissimo Chiang Kai-shek, whose wife was an American. He had been the manager of Firestone Company in Bombay before taking up this assignment. He had organised the import of tyres for China from South Africa through Rangoon. These tyres were brought to Rangoon and the Chinese would take them to Kunming in their own trucks. He suggested that Hugh take up the handling of this business for which he would receive a substantial fee. All that was needed was a godown in which to store the tyres after they were unloaded from the ship, till they were picked up by the Chinese trucks. There was no investment required. Again Hugh's lady luck was at work! Gradually, in addition to supplying tyres for the Chinese, Hugh started importing tyres on his own account for sale in Burma. The railway was still not organised and most transport of goods was by truck. Roads were in poor condition which increased the demand for tyres. Tyres commanded a very high premium and Hugh really made good money. Two more sons added to Hugh's family in Rangoon.

Gradually, the Burmese government became influenced by the Chinese communist policy. This resulted in a fairly strong 'Burman only' policy. One day, one of the senior ministers of the Burma government asked Hugh directly in Burmese 'Are you a Burman?' This was an indication that his days of successful business were over, so he decided to slowly wind down and get his money out. Hugh, his family and sisters left Burma in 1957, came to Belgaum and later settled in Bangalore.

*

A J D'Cruz's eldest son, Victor, after being a Lieutenant Colonel in the military service during the war in Burma, became the Chief Medical Officer of the Kachin State of Burma and later an Assistant Director of Medical Services in that country on his reversion to civil service. His second son, who had joined the Forest Service, was the Forest Officer of the Andaman Islands in the Bay of Bengal.

*

After independence in 1948, the government of Myanmar instituted rigid restrictions on Indian migration. The Union Citizenship Act of 1948 caused thousands of Indians unwilling or unable to adopt Burmese citizenship to return to India. Many became citizens; others applied, but for various reasons the decision to grant citizenship was delayed, while some Indians sat on the fence and were later declared stateless.

The Indian population of the country was substantially reduced in the 1960s, when 100,000 Indians were repatriated as part of a programme aimed at increasing the wealth and holdings of Myanmar nationals. The presence of so many Indians, with their thrift and industry, and their lower standards of living, caused a good deal of unrest in Burmese minds. On the other hand, the racial hostility of the Burmans and the military regime with its discriminatory laws against foreigners, especially Indians, created paranoia among the Burmese-Indian community and also among the Anglo-Indians. As many as 500,000 persons are said to have left Myanmar between 1962 and 1971. The waves of repatriation continued till the 1980s.

Indians left in Burma are mostly impoverished. They have tried to assimilate to the norms and standards of Burmese society. They have also adopted Burmese names to avoid discrimination.

Chapter 11

Post-script—A Granddaughter's Story

Finally, the story of my family.

It was the 1960s. As a young girl, I would watch my grandfather Louis Jose Vas, LJV, sitting silently in his armchair looking out the window at the traffic passing on the Main Road in Taunggyi, Burma, and try to imagine him as a teenager leaving his home in Goa many, many years ago, travelling to a strange land with little or no money or belongings. What were his feelings? What exciting or fearful experiences did he have on the voyage and later in Burma? Did he have friends? What kind of man was his father, Santana Vas, of whom we know nothing, except that he brought LJV to a certain point in Burma and then for some reason that family history does not record, let him fend for himself? My grandfather was a man of few words, not the story-telling type, and he did not like us to bother him with questions, so I never asked and whatever I learnt about him was told by my father and uncles. But even his sons do not know much about his early days in Burma.

Papa, as we all called LJV, had initially come with his father, Santana Salvador Vas, to Burma when he was just fourteen years old. That was sometime during the last decade of the nineteenth century. No one knows exactly when, but the story is that he ventured from the plains of Burma to the Shan hills of Taunggyi ('big mountain') which is a quaint, serene hill station nestled on a plateau.

We were also told that it was a long elephant ride up the mountains for young LJV. He was in all probability the only Goan in Taunggyi at that time. A handful of Indian businessmen (Punjabis, Marwaris and Bengalis) must have been his first companions among the Shans and other hill tribes that lived there. I can only assume that he must have felt quite alone in Taunggyi which was so unlike Goa. For one thing, there was not a single Catholic church or chapel in the whole area. So, when an Italian missionary priest came to the little town, LJV was the one who gave him hospitality in his small wooden house and helped him build the first little church in the adjoining compound.

My father, Lucio Alexander Vaz, was the first to be baptised in this church. Today St. Joseph's is a big cathedral and thousands of local and also Indian and Chinese Catholics come to worship here. There was a gradual flowering of the Catholic Church in this part of the world. LJV's great contribution to the Catholic Church was a story that my father often told us with much pride and the Pontificio Istituto Missioni Estere (PIME or the Pontifical Institute for Foreign Missions) still acknowledge his pioneering efforts to establish Christianity in the Southern Shan State of Burma. His sons carried on the tradition of offering such assistance as they could to the clergy.

Since Burma was under British rule when LJV first arrived, many British civil and army officials were posted in Taunggyi. Sir George Scott, the Victorian adventurer, was the superintendent of the Shan states at the time, and expressed his liking for the place in his journals. Someone must have noticed the sincere and honest nature of young LJV and got him a job in the Public Works Department. He worked in the department where blueprints and drawings of plans were made. His meticulous and disciplined approach and his eagerness to improve his skills must have pleased the British and he soon became Assistant Draughtsman and later rose to be Chief Draughtsman. He worked here till the war broke out and joined again when the British recaptured Burma. Even after his retirement, he continued working in the PWD as store-keeper till the late 1950s.

During the initial years of living and working in Taunggyi, my grandfather must have found it difficult to make visits to Goa considering the time, distance and travel facilities of that era. In one of his rare visits to Saligao, Luis Jose Vaz married Natividade Mascarenhas of Sonarbath, Saligao. I admire the courage of my grandmother, Natu, as she was called. To leave home and family and follow this man into the wilderness of Burma was an act of faith and courage! In the ensuing years, they had seven sons and one daughter. It was a period of hardship and struggle, and it couldn't have been easy to bring up eight children in a strange land with strange customs, but Natu was a strong woman who stoically went through it all without complaint. She probably did not have any social life because she never picked up the local language and couldn't express herself much in English either. Most of the other Goan families lived in Rangoon, which was more than a day's journey away from the Shan State, so she had hardly any contact with them except on rare visits.

During the Second World War, they lost their home and

all their belongings in the first Japanese bombings of Taunggyi. But with hard work and great endurance they rebuilt their lives after the war. Later, when Burma gained independence from British rule, the family chose to live on in Taunggyi and the second generation gradually built up their successful careers. My father, Lucio, was the eldest son of Luis and Natividade. As a young boy he spent a few years with his paternal grandfather in Saligao, Goa, and attended Mater Dei School. He also studied in St. Peter's Christian Brothers' School in Mandalay, Burma. He joined the Public Works Department and rose to the rank of Sub-Divisional Officer. So did three of my uncles, Joe, Peter and Anthony (Sonny), not forgetting Jose Cordeiro, my father's cousin, who also worked in the PWD and retired as Executive Engineer.

My father's younger brother Alexius worked as a Revenue Officer in the Municipal Office, while Robert graduated as a medical doctor and rose to become Civil Surgeon, and Frank got his degree in agriculture and later became District Agricultural Officer. Queenie, the youngest, married John Vas in Bombay and went to live in Tanzania. The family later relocated to Goa.

My uncles Joe, Peter, Sonny and Frank came in turns to Goa, found Goan brides and took them back to Burma where they became an intrinsic part of our family. Jose Codeiro, who was like the eighth brother, also brought his Goan bride, Annie Sequeira, to Burma and his family was regarded as one of the Vaz families. Robert married a local Shan nurse. We lived in different parts of the Shan State but every Christmas and Easter we would all gather at the family home in Taunggyi. We young cousins eagerly looked forward to these times of togetherness when there was so much noise and fun. LJV must have been proud of the successful, happy family he had established.

The family also went through some traumatic incidents. In the 1950s, Uncle Joe, who was posted in Kengtung near the Thai border in the Eastern Shan State, was shot at and killed in an ambush by insurgents while inspecting the roads and bridges in that area. His widow, Grace, and their two children came to live with my grandparents in Taunggyi. Uncle Sonny, too, was ambushed on the outskirts of Kengtung while on a work assignment, but luckily he escaped with only a bullet in his thigh. The bullet could not be removed and it remained in his body for over two decades, until he died in Goa. My mother, my two brothers and I were also attacked by dacoits in Kutkai near the China border in the Northern Shan State and received severe injuries.

My grandparents lived through all this, but never wanted to repatriate to India as they regarded Burma as their home. It was only after my grandfather passed away that my grandmother, my uncles and their families decided to return to Goa. Their decision to return in 1966 was influenced by the changing scenario in Burma. The military government had nationalised schools, colleges, businesses, and banks and the future was looking bleak, especially for the children of non-Burmese people. Leaving behind all the comforts of Burma and starting all over again in Goa with young children wasn't very easy. Each family unit had to try and establish themselves, to build houses, to bring up young children in a strange homeland, while the children too had to adjust to new schools, new friends and a new culture. My family could not come away with the rest, but did so more than a decade later. But now every family is doing well for themselves and another generation has come up.

My grandfather, Louis Jose Vas, lies buried in his adopted hometown of Taunggyi in Burma. My grandmother died and was buried in Saligao, Goa. The rest of the large clan that they established continues to live in Goa or has scattered to other parts of the world.

Migration all over again!

PART II: OTHER VOICES

Chapter 1

An Excerpt from *White Butterflies* by Colin McPhedran

In his moving and well-written book, *White Butterflies* (published by Pandanus Publishers in 2002), Colin McPhedran narrates his experiences of the exodus from Burma to India during the Second World War. He has a chapter on the aerial bombing of the last airport in Burma by the Japanese which ended the efforts of the British to ferry refugees to India by air.

Like thousands of stranded Europeans, Eurasians and Indians, Colin had no option but to trek the long dangerous route across the Hukaung Valley to India. Besides the physical hardships encountered on the way, Colin suffered the death of his mother, elder brother and sister and reached India alone, desperately weak and ill.

His chapter on the bombing of Myitkyina airport is a most detailed and graphic first-hand account. It is included in this book courtesy of Newsouth Publishing Australia, who hold the copyright.

Another day arrived and hopes of a plane arriving to pick us up rose. At mid-morning when our family along with thousands of other refugees was busy preparing a meal, we heard the drone of an aircraft. Immediately there were shouts from the crowd; shouts of hope and joy that we might be rescued and flown out of the war zone.

'The plane could well be an enemy aircraft,' Robert cautioned.

He was mistaken. It was indeed a friendly plane and as it came into view we identified it.

'Look! It's just like the one that came yesterday!'

Indeed, it was a cargo plane similar to the one that had taken off with the remnants of the British Raj the previous day. The crowd surged on to the apron of the strip and waited for it to circle and land. Soldiers armed with rifles appeared from nowhere and took up positions at the point where the pilot would stop. There was much screaming and yelling as the armed men threatened to shoot anybody breaking rank.

As the plane came to a stop, the cargo hatch was thrown open and the soldiers formed up and proceeded to let people in. Families were separated in the rush and I saw small children sitting on the ground wailing for their mothers who seemingly had already entered the plane. It was nightmarish and despite the throb of the engines still running, the sound of human voices was deafening.

I looked up at the front of the plane and saw the pilot and his crew half-out of the open window waving at the people to hurry along. The pilot, whom I could see clearly, was clothed in a singlet and he had a head of the reddest hair I had ever seen. He was just a youngster and the look of urgency on his face made me think that he was aware of some impending danger from the enemy who were just a few miles east of the town.

My mother and sister were bundled aboard but a surly soldier barred Robert and me.

'Only women and children are allowed on,' he said.

There was no point in arguing with a madman armed with a rifle. So my brother and I waited to wave goodbye and signalled to my mother who was still standing in the opened hatch.

'We will walk across the mountains and meet you in India,' we mouthed and tried to convey the message in sign language. She shook her head as if to say there was no way she would go without us and scrambled off the plane, pulling my sister with her. As she did so, she picked up a young child who seemed to be holding its arms out to somebody on the plane and lifted the crying toddler into the hatch-way.

It only took us a minute to realise that our hopes of getting on were dashed, so we regrouped and moved away from the milling mob and the stifling heat, back to our campsite about 150 yards from the strip on higher ground. In many ways, it was a relief to get away from the dangers of a panicking crowd. We chatted while we watched the final closing of the plane's cargo hatch from our grandstand position.

The engines roared as the pilot made to move off with an overloaded plane. It moved slowly and turned to taxi to the far end of the strip. At this moment I was surprised to see two smaller planes at low level heading straight at the landing strip. Their engines could not be heard above the roar of the larger plane's engines.

'They're Japanese fighter bombers!' I shouted.

The faces of the two-man crew were plainly visible and

the red ball of the rising sun painted on the fuselage stood out against the camouflaged body of the rest of the plane.

The bomber flew over the aircraft loaded with refugees at tree-top level, before banking and making another run at the bigger plane. It opened fire with all guns blazing and scored a direct hit which burst the tyres of the cargo plane, immobilised it and left it lurching on its side. The second fighter that followed close behind unloaded its bombs which hurtled down to explode directly on the stricken aircraft. We watched in horror as people fell out of the flaming wreck. There was nothing we could do but witness the slaughter.

The two planes flew back and forth for what seemed a long time, time enough for my brother Robert to display his anger by picking up his old Enfield rifle and having a shot at the planes. I too fired a few rounds at the low-flying planes until my mother screamed at us.

'Quick! Take shelter! The planes are attacking the people skirting the strip!'

At this point, my mother, sister and brother jumped into the well nearby while I ran behind the only trees in sight. With the plane full of refugees in flames, the Japanese aircraft moved off the direct flight and dropped a couple of bombs perilously close to us. I could feel the blast and watched the planes climb and head away. The other three came running over and gave me a dressing-down for exposing myself to the attack. Mother put her arms round me and in a flash drew back and exclaimed, 'You've been wounded!'

I had sustained a wound on my right shoulder and a few minor shrapnel shots down the right side of my body.

'It's nothing serious,' I said. I had not even felt it during the excitement of the attack. At that moment a middle-aged Anglo-Indian man came over and began to abuse Robert and me for shooting at the Japanese planes.

'Such stupid behaviour could have attracted the pilots and diverted their attention in this direction. We could have all been killed,' he said. He continued to berate us until he eyed Robert with his hands on the offending weapon.

The plane on the strip was still alight and clouds of smoke continued to pour out. People were screaming and bodies were scattered all over the ground. There was nothing anyone could do. Nobody possessed any first-aid equipment since we were all travelling with the barest essentials.

My mother was visibly saddened. 'This looks like the end. The strip has been damaged to such an extent that no plane could possibly land there safely now. Our only option now is to take the long walk back to the township, find a spot to spend the night and talk over our plans for the trek out.'

Hundreds of people joined the long line of desperately saddened families. I still remember the eerie quietness of the walk. Nobody seemed to utter a word and everybody seemed intent on just following the footsteps of those ahead. Only once, late in the afternoon did we break rank. A plane flew overhead and, suspecting it was a Japanese plane about to offload its cargo of bombs, the long line of weary walkers dived into the deep drains that are a feature of any town or village in tropical countries.

The road was treeless, which seemed unusual. Perhaps the adjoining land was cultivated for crops, hence the treelessness; I did not know. I did not want to know. I knew there was a long walk of hundreds of miles ahead, no matter what the decision was about the route. The makeshift bandages on my leg and shoulder were steeped in blood. The superficial wounds did not impede my walk, but the flies were having a feast and I wished the sun would soon set, encouraging them to rest somewhere else.

Chapter 2

Helen the Legend and Jerry the Writer

Award-winning poet and writer, Jerry Pinto, interweaves fragments of a personal family story and a part of his poem into the story of Helen, the legendary Bollywood dancer.

'…a slit-eyed teenage girl of Spanish-Burmese ancestry arrived in Bombay, having escaped from Burma. The legs that carried her through the jungles of the Northeast were later to take Helen to fame.'
—*The Hundred Luminaries of Hindi Cinema*
by Dinesh Raheja and Jitendra Kothari

When [my book] *Helen: The Life and Times of a Bollywood H-Bomb* (Penguin India) came out, I was often asked why. By the time I was writing about her, she was in semi-retirement. Most journalists thought of her as the original item girl. I did not think so. I thought she was a very important ingredient in the construction of our cinema. I believed that the Helen figure had something to say about cosmopolitanism, something to say about insularity too. I believed that on her lissome form, Bollywood's best had tacked tacky outfits galore, but they had also pinned their beliefs about who they were and how they constructed the Other. Anything could be said about her.

Lagta hai inki maa ne bahut Chinese khaana khaaya hai. (Her mother must have eaten a great deal of Chinese food.) runs a line from the film *Pyaar Hi Pyaar*. Vijay (Dharmendra), the hero, is referring to Helen, whom he has just met. *Mera naam Chin-Chin-Choo* (My name is Chin-Chin-Choo) she sings in her breakthrough number in *Howrah Bridge*. She could be a queen, she could be a princess, she could be a tribal or a fairy. She was always fascinating but there was another element to that story.

My mother talked of Burma infrequently. It was not a memory she relished. I used some of it in a poem that I published in *Asylum and Other Poems* (Allied Publishers). Here it is:

EXILED HOME FROM BURMA

I
'We must leave behind
The coal mine and the teak plantation
The trays of sweets sent by debtors
And the memory of morning massages,'
Said my grandmother. Her ears,
Preternaturally sharp, could hear
Hitler goose-stepping (by proxy)
Through melted forests of teak.

II
'By all the laws of navigation, ma'am
A lighter ship may travel faster,'

Said the captain and went hunting.
He found a piano; a mastodon mired
In Mozart, it was trapped quickly
And drowned well.
Once the Shwe Dagon ignored
Scales played by dutiful fingers.
Now fan-tailed fish lodge in its shell.

III
'Bombs have no eyes.
They will not see it is my Johnny,
A good boy who took his mother dancing.
But God has ears that we can storm,
And my Johnny has strong legs.'
Said my great-grandmother,
her brood gathered around her.

IV
Orange sweets may fail you
Melting glutinously in fat-necked bottles
Orange peel will not.
Dry—it will dispel the nausea of exile
Wet—it will spurt rage into the eyes
of a wet-lipped sailor
Attracted by the smell of a girl's first bleeding.

I'm sorry. You came in looking for a story about Helen and you ended up with a story about Jerry.

    Time to refocus.

*

Helen Richardson was born on July 14, 1938 or 1939. (All these dates are uncertain since they vary from telling to telling.). Her mother was Marlene, a half-Spanish half-Burmese woman who married a Frenchman. After his death, Marlene married again, a British officer this time, whose name Helen took, becoming Helen Richardson. The family was stationed in Burma when the Second World War broke out. Japan joined the Axis powers in September 1940 and by December 1941, Japanese troops had invaded Burma. By May 1942, the conquest of Burma was complete, which means the retreat of the British troops and non-indigenous British subjects must have begun earlier that year. The women and children were sent by boat to what was then Calcutta. The men walked.

Marlene and her family had left it too late to get on to any of the boats. They were forced to walk from Burma to Assam. Helen told *Filmfare* (3 April, 1964) the story of their flight to India. It reads like a first-person account but, going by the journalistic practices of the 1960s, would probably have been an 'as told to' piece (a journalist talks to the actor and then writes it up as a first-person account):

'It was a cold December night in Rangoon. The year was 1941. Burma was being mercilessly bombed by the Japanese. Everywhere people were fleeing the country. My mother packed a few things and we went to the airport with my baby brother in mother's arms. That night, the aerodrome was bombed. Frightened and nervous, we returned home.

Life in Rangoon became unbearable for us, Father had been killed on the battlefront early in the war and there was no one to take care of us. Besides, life was insecure in the war-stricken city. When friends decided to come over to India with their families, mother agreed to join them. Then from Upper Burma began our long, gruelling trek to Assam.

I was only about three years old at that time. But I was to hear about that torturous journey often from mother.'

For weeks, she goes on to say, they trekked alternately through wilderness and 'hundreds of villages', surviving on the generosity of people, for they were penniless, with no food and few clothes. Occasionally, they met British soldiers who provided them with transport, found them refuge, 'treated our blistered feet and bruised bodies and fed us'. By the time they reached Dibrugarh in Assam, their group had been reduced to half. Some had fallen ill and been left behind, some had died of starvation and exposure. The survivors were admitted to the Dibrugarh hospital for treatment. 'Mother and I had been virtually reduced to skeletons and my brother's condition was critical. We spent two months in hospital. When we recovered, we moved to Calcutta.'

Helen spoke of the trauma again to Khalid Mohamed, then editor of *Filmfare*, of walking and running for months, of ducking bombs, of her mother miscarrying a baby girl on the way, of seeing dozens of people killed. So traumatised was she that her hands would shake for the rest of her life, especially when she heard sirens or saw anything that reminded her of those times.

In Nasreen Munni Kabir's television special, *Helen: Always In Step*, she said: 'It's surprising, I was so young but I can still remember a moment when in the middle of the night we were running out of the house and we passed a place where a bomb must have fallen. It was a shop and there was hair and blood and [bits of] skull on the wall. I still have that dream sometimes. It's very vivid in my mind.'

Returning once more to the *Filmfare* story:

'Life in Calcutta was no bed of roses. Mother, a trained nurse, slogged at odd jobs to feed us. Despite her best efforts to save my ailing brother, he died [of smallpox]. Mother felt the blow deeply. Calcutta now stifled her…After living for some years in Hyderabad and Deolali [in northern Maharashtra], we moved to Bombay in 1947. Here life really began for me. So far, I had known only a rolling-stone existence.'

*

Thus Helen Richardson, now Helen Khan, was one of the survivors of one of the greatest migrations in human history. In the epigraph at the start of this piece, Raheja and Kothari mention those legs. Helen herself would attribute their shapeliness and their strength to the trek through the forest, undertaken at such an early age.

My grandfather trekked through the same jungles and came out the other side his hair white; my mother and her mother came by boat. For years afterwards, we would hear fragments of the story and now many more have begun to emerge after I read the first edition of this book. There are more stories hidden in those forests and we are losing some every day as the last survivors are taken from us by the relentless march of time. As we lose memory, we lose humanity. And this is a loss we can ill afford at this time in our evolution.

Chapter 3

Benegal Dinker Rao: Barefoot from Burma to India, 1942

Benegal Dinker Rao was born in 1917 in Rangoon, graduated from the University of Rangoon in 1938 and joined the Education Ministry of the Government of Burma. After his walk from Burma to India in 1942, he joined the Refugee Government of Burma in Simla. In 1943, he joined the Indian Army Ordnance Corps. He resigned from the Corps in 1952 to work for a Calcutta-based British engineering company, from which he retired as Marketing Director in 1978 and moved to Pune, where he lived until his death.

Arvind Benegal, a nephew of Benegal Dinker, wrote this story based on his uncle's clear and precise oral accounts of the events of 1942.

The Japanese Air Force first bombed Rangoon (now Yangon) on December 23, 1941. Then again on December 25th, this time with incendiary bombs. Burma (now Myanmar) was part of the British Empire, and was now part of the Second World War. Soon after, the Japanese Army invaded Burma.

I was twenty-four years old, living in Rangoon as an

employee of the Government of Burma. My family consisted of my mother, Kalyani Bai, and two younger brothers, Sumitra and Ramesh. We also had with us Madiman Dutta, eighty years old, a faithful elder servant who had been attached to our family for so long that he was treated as a family member.

Most Indian families left Burma for India as soon as possible; they travelled by sea from Rangoon to Calcutta (now Kolkata). However, I could not leave Burma because I was classified as an 'essential' government employee who had to stay on in Rangoon. Nevertheless, I did not want to expose my family to the ongoing bombing in Rangoon. So I arranged to send my mother and brothers to Bassein, in southwest Burma on the Bay of Bengal, which was not being bombed.

By mid-January 1942, the Japanese were bombing Rangoon night and day. Food became scarce; law and order broke down. My friend M.G. Mankikar had stayed behind in Rangoon as he too was classified as an 'essential' government employee. He and I moved to the suburban bungalow of Dr P.G. Gollerkeri, where we dug an air-raid trench, and stocked it with some drinking water and a little food.

Soon, we were forced to live in the trench as the bombings increased in frequency and intensity. During one air-raid, when I was out in the open, en route to an air-raid shelter, a bomb landed a few yards away from me. I threw myself flat on the ground and thought it was the end. But the bomb did not explode—there was just a huge crater where it had landed.

Before my mother and brothers left Rangoon, my mother

had fried a jarful of mirsange kachris, (fried dried chillies), one of my favourite condiments. One day in late February 1942, after two days of starvation, I swallowed the kachris with a few drops of rationed water. You can imagine the painful consequence to my digestive system!

When Singapore fell to the Japanese in February 1942, we knew that Rangoon would fall soon. We sent word to our families to go overland to India via Arakan and Chittagong, which is what they did. By the end of February 1942, the British and Indian troops left Rangoon, and the Government of Burma officially moved to Maymyo, a hill station on the western Shan Hills which extend to Yunnan in China.

Maymyo is a plateau, ringed on three sides by mountains; the fourth (open) side is connected to Mandalay by rail and road. The Japanese had driven through Yunnan and were on the mountains ringing Maymyo, taking shots at anything that moved. So we spent the daytime in trenches, coming out only at night. There was no electric power at all, but even a lit cigarette or a torch light could attract sniper fire.

The Government of Burma declared itself defunct in mid-April 1942, with the idea that a small Government-in-exile would be set up in India, perhaps in Delhi or Simla. Government servants were told that they could either remain 'as-is where-is' and surrender to the Japanese, or could make their way to India at their own risk. Mainmath and I decided to try and make it to India, fairly certain that our families were safely settled there.

On April 21, 1942, Mainmath and I started our trek from Maymyo to India. The distance is about 520 kilometres (320 miles) as the crow flies—and much more than this on the ground. We did it in thirty-four days by whatever means we could: walking, by raft, and an occasional lift from someone in a motor vehicle.

When we reached Mandalay, the city was burning. The Japanese had firebombed it that morning. The fire was devastating because all the houses were made of wood. In the Mandalay railway station yard, we found ourselves surrounded by burning debris, and soldiers and civilians dead or dying from cholera or black water fever. We were dying of thirst. The only safe water available was from the boilers of railway engines. The water was full of coal ash and wood ash—but we drank it as if it was nectar from Heaven itself.

In Mandalay, we came across an Indian Army unit of the Survey of India. Fortunately for us, the officer-in-charge was a Benegal Pandurang! He gave us some bread from his unit's rations. His unit had been asked to destroy all records, arms, equipment, and to get to India by the Mogaung-Ledo route up the Irrawaddy. Mainmath and I planned to take the Tamu route to Manipur up the Chindwin River.

From Mandalay, we trekked to Kalewa, which is located at the confluence of the Chindwin and Myittha rivers. From Kalewa, instead of walking, we would float on the Chindwin River on improvised rafts—tree branches tied with anything that could hold them together. But, even before we took off, we were looted by Burmese/Chin dacoits, who took away everything we had, leaving Mainmath and me in our vests and shorts and nothing else.

There were other India-bound families along with us on rafts on the Chindwin River. Some distance from Kalewa, the river flows through a gorge with sheer white cliffs. The monsoon had just broken in Upper Burma and a tidal-bore type of flood came down the river, lifting our rafts a good 50–100 feet. One raft had a family with two children. They bore the brunt of the flood-wave and the children were flung into recesses halfway up the cliffs. The raft with the parents came down to pre-flood levels and uncontrollably floated downstream. Birds—either eagles or hawks—were circling and pecking at the terrified children. A ghastly end...

Once we reached Kalemyo, we had to walk—barefoot, as we had no shoes. Our first target was to reach Tamu on the Burma-Manipur border, and then onto Palel. Between Tamu and Palel, when Mainmath and I were plodding in torrential rain, we came to an abandoned cattle shelter with a half-torn thatch roof. We were too exhausted to walk any more. When we lay down in the slush, we realised that there was a half-bare woman and a naked child lying there moaning. But we were so tired that we fell asleep. When I woke up, I could not move because the child had its arms around my feet. To my horror, the child was dead. Both mother and child had smallpox. Somehow, God saved me from the contagion.

From Palel we walked to Kanglatongbi. On the road to Kanglatongbi, which was used by the British army and Indian troops as a retreat route, we passed many British soldiers lying with glazed eyes—victims of cholera or black water fever. Some had passed away; others were about to die. Most of them were in their teens, and wanted us to convey their last thoughts to their mothers and sisters. But we had no paper or pens to write down their whispered addresses.

At Kanglatongbi, Army trucks were bringing supplies

from Kohima in Nagaland, and returning with wounded and sick soldiers. In one three-tonne truck, some jawans (soldiers) of a Sikh Light Infantry unit said there was space for Mainmath and me, if we could climb in. In helping me, a burly Sikh stamped heavily on my feet with his ammunition boots. Sheer agony! Thereafter, on this journey, my feet were a mass of open flesh, dried blood, pus and dirt.

From Kohima, we got to the Manipur Road Railway Station (Dimapur), where Army medical personnel tried to ease my pain. After another week, I was sent to Calcutta, then with an Army Medical Corps Unit to Bombay (now Mumbai) by train. All the while, I had high fever, later diagnosed as black water. In Bombay, Kamala (my cousin) and Mangesh Nadgar traced me. They took me to their residence, Fl Anandashram, where they cleaned me, and then took me to a hospital.

EPILOGUE

After sixty-one years, I still use Fl Anandashram as my sanctuary on my visits to Bombay.

My mother, my brothers, and our eighty-year-old family retainer managed to make their way to Magwe in Central Burma, just ahead of a Japanese forward unit. A senior British official was to be evacuated from there, and a Royal Air Force plane was sent to rescue him. The pilot was Biju Patnaik, who later became a leading politician and the Chief Minister of Orissa. The plane landed on time but the British officer had not reached Magwe. So Patnaik said he would pick up Indian ladies and the sick, and take them to Chittagong. My mother and our family servant were airlifted, but both my brothers were left behind.

All of us suffered heavily during the next few years during the war. And, yet, a short time after the war was over, our family had bounced back, and we went on to live normal, productive lives in which we made our contributions to India's well-being and development.

My brother Sumitra remained in Burma. When Netaji Chandra Bose came there, Sumitra joined the Indian National Army (INA), which Netaji had founded to fight the British for India's independence. Sumitra was in one of the first batches of trainees to undergo military training. He rose to be a personal aide of Netaji in Burma. As a result of the training, he became a crack shot with the revolver. When the British regained Burma in 1945, he was taken prisoner of war, and was lodged in Insein Jail (where Aung San Suu Kyi was held in 2004). He was released after the INA trials were over in India and came to India in 1947.

My brother Ramesh, who had also remained in Burma, joined the INA as well. Netaji selected him personally to be a Tokyo cadet for intensive aviation training at the Japanese Imperial Aviation Academy, Tokyo, and to be the core of a would-be INA Air Wing. He, too, returned to India in 1946 as a prisoner of war. Later, he joined the Indian Air Force, had a very adventurous career, and was honoured first with the Ati Vishishtha Seva Medal, which is awarded by the President of India to recognise 'distinguished service of an exceptional order' to all ranks of the armed forces, later with the Maha Vir Chakra, the second highest military decoration in India, which is awarded for acts of conspicuous gallantry in the presence of the enemy, whether on land, at sea or in the air.

Chapter 4

Shakuntala's Story

This story is taken from the book *Bravo Mum* written by Shakuntala Peter and published in a beautiful hand-crafted edition, with a handloom sari cover, by Writers Workshop in 2004. This is a condensed version of her story of the Second World War in Burma.

My father, Solomon Ramalingam, was born in Madras, India, in 1892, studied in India and later in the USA, where he did his masters degree in History. He went to Burma where he was appointed as a lecturer in Mandalay College which was then under Rangoon University. My mother, Daisy David, and my father made an ideal couple and they were the most loving and devoted parents to us four siblings. Our lives were full of fun and laughter till our happy world came crashing down when my father contracted typhoid fever and passed away in July 1941.

Mother's younger sister Annie and her husband Dr Stephen Paul took us into their home in Mokpalin in Lower Burma although they had three daughters of their own to care for. In December, my aunt Annie, who was oblivious of the impending Japanese attack, took my younger brother Shivaji and me by train to Rangoon to buy toys and gifts for Christmas. We excitedly set out for the journey which would take just a few hours.

Suddenly we were jolted from our thoughts and chatter by a loud explosion. This was followed by one booming sound and then another. As we approached the city, the thunderous sounds became louder and continued for some time. The engine driver halted the train and the passengers rushed down into the open green fields. We looked up in amazement and witnessed a strange and terrible sight. A number of planes were circling Rangoon, swooping down and bombing the place. We could see smoke and flames shooting up, accompanied by a loud explosive sound every time a plane dived down and dropped a bomb. People around us started wailing, screaming and shouting, worried about their loved ones in Rangoon.

The driver blew the horn, made everyone get back on the train and hastily beat a retreat to Mokpalin. We had just witnessed the first bombing of Burma. It was the morning of 23 December 1941.

As the war progressed, people began to flee Burma. We could not trek out as we were seven children below the age of twelve in our group. My uncle's father, Rao Bahadur, (the title he was bestowed for his good work and innovation) Dr Samuel Paul arranged for us to move to Myanaung, a town on the Irrawaddy riverside. Uncle put us on a train to Myanaung and all our belongings into a wagon. We later heard that all our bags and boxes were thrown out at the railway station in Prome because the British army needed the wagon for their things. We lost everything except our clothes and my mother's sewing machine, which she treasured because it had been a gift from my father.

At Myanaung we were met by our grand-uncle. The house we were to live in was barely furnished, with a small compound. We missed our old, spacious, comfortable house and, to make matters worse, my mother had to leave for Mandalay to get my father's insurance money from the bank which was about to close down. My uncle too had to go on duty and attend to the wounded soldiers as far north as Myitkyina.

In the meantime the Japanese army was advancing towards our town. We were so afraid of the Japanese soldiers who looked like angry young men, with slit eyes and round stern faces. They inflicted a reign of terror, burning people, torturing them in different ways if they suspected them of being pro-British or pro-Chinese. We heard whispers of massacres, beheadings and shootings. Even petty crimes and littering of public places was punished by lashings in the market place. Books or any writing in English were burnt in bonfires. We had to hide our encyclopaedias and the Union Jack flag which my brother put in a box and buried in a hole in the ground. We spoke only Burmese because the Japanese punished people who used the English language. They did not carry much supplies so they took food, medicines and whatever they wanted by force from the local people.

My grand-uncle was in charge of us. He was a very strict disciplinarian and at seventy-nine felt the burden of looking after all of us. He believed that my mother and uncle were both dead and he called Shivaji and me to tell us, 'Now that you are parentless, you will have to take over the job of looking after your sisters, Shakuntala. And you, Shivaji, will have to learn a trade. I know a watch repairer who will teach you.'

He made me scrub pots and pans, wash clothes, clean the house and look after the children. He made the barber cut our hair so short that we looked like little prisoners. We girls cried so hard that day. We were already so shattered and could not bear the thought that we had lost our darling mother. I, as the eldest, had to console the younger ones and then go and cry my heart out in the next room. Shivaji and I were as terrified and confused as the younger ones but tried to be strong. My aunt was quiet and depressed with no news from her husband and elder sister, whose children she was responsible for now. It was a month since my mother had left and money kept for a fortnight was almost exhausted. We had just one meal of rice and vegetables a day and the evening meal was conjee, soft-boiled rice. It was painful to have the same tasteless food every day but hunger made us consume it.

One day the Allies dropped pamphlets asking civilians to move away from places like the railway station, the wharf, factories, etc. because they were going to drop bombs in these areas. Shivaji picked up and brought home one of these pamphlets. We were living near the railway station and decided to shift to a house some distance away. This move made us so thankful because we escaped certain death and injury when the station was bombed intensely. The Allies also began to machine-gun the wharf and the boats plying in the river. They must have realised that the Japanese soldiers were hiding in them. Planes came in low and dropped bombs. The Post and Telegraph Office, other offices, banks, mills and factories were damaged and the sounds were terrifying. Buildings and trees were burning and all this continued for many days. The Japanese countered with anti-aircraft guns. We did not experience direct hits but we heard of the sufferings of those who were injured. When we saw tiny specks of the planes getting larger and closer we would run into the trench and cower.

We were not allowed to leave the house and lived through a traumatic period of fear-filled days. Shivaji was the only one who left the house for a few hours every day to get vegetables and we waited with dread till he returned. We trembled with horror when we thought of what Mother was going through but could not talk about it because granduncle forbade us to. He was convinced that she was dead while we felt in our hearts that she would return.

When she did return at the end of June with my uncle, it seemed like a miracle and our joy knew no bounds. It was next to impossible to travel safely across the war-torn country but they found us, even though we had shifted to a different house. [See the next chapter for her story]. We were able to withstand three-and-a-half more years of the war. We still suffered food shortages and other hardships, but our loved ones were back and nothing else mattered.

My uncle, Dr Stephen Paul, had great compassion and tenderness for the suffering. After every bombardment, he would run out with his bag slung over his shoulder to care for the wounded and sick. Although he did not have many medicines, he carried something to staunch the flow of blood and something to ease the pain or clean wounds. He walked long distances and worked tirelessly without hope of payment. He helped many to survive and those who died in his hands were calmed and comforted. He was called the Sadhu Doctor because he would run out barefoot any time, day or night, to attend to the injured.

Netaji Subhas Chandra Bose, the great Indian freedom fighter, believed that the Japanese could help India fight the British and attain independence from colonial rule. He built up the Indian National Army in Burma. At the end of 1943 we saw him and some of his followers march through the streets of Myanaung shouting slogans and calling for people to join them. We rushed to the road that was lined with people. We saw Netaji in the middle of the first row, calling loudly to Indians among the crowd, '*Bhai aur Bhaino Chalo Dilli.*' (Brothers and sisters lets march to Delhi). Another slogan we heard was, 'Young men of India, join us to attain Poorna Swaraj (complete freedom) for our country.' The people shouted in return, '*Netaji ki jai!*'

Many Indians became fired with patriotism with his call to fight for the nation. The INA in Burma was very enthusiastic if not well trained. It is ironic that Indians in the INA fought Indians in the Allied Armed forces. Subhas Chandra Bose lost many of his men in battle as well as to malaria and dysentery. But his courage and patriotism will always be remembered.

One day the area neighbouring our house was bombed and it became imperative that we leave. We had heard that the Francis brothers owned a large piece of land and they had in their bigness of heart permitted people to come and build their own small houses around their residence. It was comparatively safer than places elsewhere because it was hidden from the sight of planes by the thick bamboo and other leafy trees that grew in abundance. We built a long, low barrack-like house with slit bamboo flooring, mat-woven walls and thatch roofs. There were about thirty families living in this compound and we developed friendships which made us relaxed and happy. The grown-ups too were glad to see us playing and having fun in the spacious garden. We called this place 'The Garden' and it was safe because the Japanese soldiers and police had no enmity with the Indians in Burma and left us alone. We did not live in so much fear as we had in the previous year. However, we still went through shortages of food and other essential items. And we knew the bombing and horrors of the war were still going on nearby. We reared ducks and chickens for food, tried growing vegetables and Mother used the sewing machine to convert saris and longyis into clothing for us. She also taught us various subjects so our minds were not idle.

Necessity made us try different ways to earn money. I learnt to knit and sold one of my sports shirts made with cotton yarn for Rs 400. Shivaji used to buy biscuits and sell them for a small profit. Mother too tried her hand at doing some business. It did not bring in much income but Mother sometimes sold her beautiful gold ornaments and we managed to be less dependent on our aunt and uncle. They had another baby girl while we were staying in The Garden which became a joy for all of us, but the much-loved baby contracted a stomach infection and died when she was nine months old. Grand-uncle too died soon after, with a similar stomach ailment. He had been a pillar of strength and support to us and left a big void in our lives.

We were fortunate to have a loving and talented family.

Shakuntala's Story

My mother not only worked herself to the bone to fulfil our physical needs but also taught us poetry and strengthened our spirits with prayer and faith and trust in a loving God. Uncle Stephen was a man of few words but very patient and kind. He spent long hours tending to the sick and wounded but never felt it was a burden. He was also good with his hands and taught Shivaji the rudiments of carpentry. We learnt a great deal from his example of selfless service to others and also from the clear and level-headed advice he gave us. My aunt staged plays, taught us songs and rhymes and gave us children what we needed badly, a lighter slice of life. She also tried her best to give us a treat on our birthdays.

All of us learnt the Japanese national songs and we invited the Japanese officers to our concerts. They jumped up and lustily sang along with us.

In the beginning of 1944 we saw the use of new aircraft by the British. One day we witnessed a duel in the sky between a Spitfire and a Japanese Zero. The pilots swooped down low and were circling each other like opponents in a wrestling match when suddenly the Spitfire gained height with a swift turn and began shooting at the Japanese plane from behind. The Japanese plane was torn apart and burning. The pilot tried to dart away on a wing with the other wing in flames. It began twisting and falling like a leaf in the wind, the engines still roaring till it was enveloped in flames and fell to the ground a little distance from where we were staying. The Japanese pilot had managed to escape by parachuting before the plane disintegrated. A large number of people including us rushed to see the fallen smouldering plane which was being cordoned off by the Japanese soldiers while the Spitfire had flown away intact with its pilot.

By May 1945 the Burmese Army had organised themselves into a powerful group. They killed thousands of Japanese soldiers and the Allies came with their Mosquito, Spitfire and Thunderbolt aircraft, chasing the fleeing soldiers, killing many thousands more. Many Japanese soldiers also committed hara-kiri, killing themselves with their own swords as they felt this was more honourable than being taken prisoner. The Allied planes dropped food, clothing and pamphlets.

But our troubles were not yet over. On April 8, 1945, a group of Burmese soldiers belonging to the Burmese National Army fired at a train carrying retreating Japanese soldiers and killed some of them. The enraged Japanese rushed out of the train ready to shoot at anyone. We were watching from nearby and had to run and hide in a trench. My uncle had the foresight to move us under our house as he felt the trench would be searched for the culprits who had attacked the train. He was right. While we were crouching uncomfortably among the two-feet-high stilts which supported the floor, Japanese soldiers climbed into the trench and also looked into our house but luckily they didn't see us hiding under the house. They were raving and ranting and we were so relieved that we had had such a narrow escape.

People were now fleeing the towns and going to the villages. It was time for us too to leave for the jungle. Now that the Japanese were retreating, the Burmans did not fear the law. They were hungry and in a state of despair and they resented the Indians and Chinese because they seemed better off than them. Many of them, wielding sharp dahs (knives), turned dacoit and attacked people, ransacked houses and shops and even raped and killed. Being a group of Indians at The Garden, we felt we were open targets. We hired a bullock cart and piled it with a few essential items: clothes, pots and pans, bedding and some groceries. Uncle stayed behind and Mother, Aunt Annie and we seven children climbed onto the cart. We were heading to an unknown fate without the support of Uncle and all the friends at The Garden. We were filled with anxiety but Mother made us pray and Aunty told us we should thank God for keeping us unharmed during the past terrible years. Sheila, who was five, did not feel the anxiety and asked, 'Are we going on a picnic?' which made us all laugh and eased the tension.

The cartman took us to a village called Kanchindown and stopped in front of a fairly large farmhouse. The Burmese couple was kind enough to let us sleep in one of their rooms during the night and Mother told them that during the day we would sit under the big mango tree so as not to disturb them. We collected twigs and cooked rice and some vegetables for our meals. We were devoid of comfort and proper food but Mother would read to us from Charlotte Bronte's *Jane Eyre* and try to entertain us. We lived at Kanchindown for one month. There were anxious days when my youngest sister, Sharola, and cousin, Sheila, had severe attacks of whooping cough and as soon as they got better we decided to return to The Garden. Uncle was there and everyone seemed to be in a joyous mood. A plane flew over one day and dropped pamphlets saying, 'Germany surrendered. War in Europe over. Japan now stands alone.' We were excited and danced with delight! No more bombings and machine-gunning, no more fear of being tortured and killed by the Japanese! We had miraculously escaped with our lives and limbs intact and were of sound minds. The war was finally over and after four years of terror and deprivation we were now free to make plans, to go back to India and live without fear and foreboding.

Chapter 5

Bravo Mum

Shakuntala titled her book *Bravo Mum* in praise and honour of her courageous mother who endured so much trauma and hardship yet was a rock for her children. Her strength, kindness, patience and unswerving faith in God comforted them and brought them safely through the horrors of the war. This account has been extracted from the book and condensed.

My mother, Daisy David, came from Dharwad, a small town in Karnataka, India. She was beautiful, educated and talented. She married my father in Madras and went with him to Burma, where we four siblings grew up amidst so much love, fun, security and comfort. My Father passed away just before the Anglo-Japanese War broke out in Burma, but Mother was our pillar of strength. She and my aunt and uncle took good care of and protected the four of us and our three young cousins through the dark and dangerous days of the bombings and Japanese occupation.

One day in March 1942, Mother decided to go to Mandalay to claim the settlement of my father's insurance policy from the Imperial Bank of India before it shut down.

We knew we desperately needed the money but it was heart-wrenching to part with Mother even for a few days; besides there was a war going on. Little did we know what dangers she would face! She travelled from Myanaung on a launch to Prome and then to Mandalay on a crowded steamer for six days, listening to fearful rumours and longing to turn back and be with us. At Mandalay she went to stay at a friend's house and since she was anxious to get news of us, she tried sending telegraph messages but they never reached us. Many friends tried to help her get in touch with us but none succeeded. Mother was lucky to get her money from the bank because a few days later, on Good Friday, 3 April, 1942, Mandalay was bombed.

All the other members of the house had gone for the church service and Mother was alone in the house, preparing a meal. Suddenly about forty Japanese bomber planes flew over and started dropping bombs on the defenceless city. The terrible explosions filled the air with deafening noises, dust and smoke but she ran through it all as fast as she could into the trench in front of the house. Alone and terrified she screamed, she cried out to God and pleaded with Him to save her for the sake of her children. The bombing continued for a long time and when the noise subsided, she crept out and saw to her horror that almost all the surrounding houses were in flames and there was smoke and dust everywhere. She rushed into the house, dragged out the suitcase with the money in it, carried it to the trench and went into the house again to get other essentials like medicines, blankets, drinking water and suddenly remembered there was an old man upstairs. She found him lying huddled in a corner of the room, trembling and weeping loudly while the fire was spreading to all the walls. She guided him out of the house just before it collapsed in flames, then she went into the trench, hastily packed a small bag with some clothes and the money and taking the old man by the hand, left the compound.

Just outside, there was a bicycle repair shop, and the owner who was bleeding profusely begged her for a few drops of water to drink. Mother gave him a drink from a pot of water on the roadside and was sad to see him at the point of death. She looked around at the carnage: dead bodies of men, women and children were strewn everywhere, people were wailing either in physical pain or for the death of their loved ones; horses and bullocks that were still attached to the carts they were pulling, were lying dead too. Bicycles, cars and trucks, twisted out of shape added to the debris. Fires continued unabated and Mother wondered where they could go for safety. To her relief a truck full of Tommies (soldiers) stopped and one of them called out, 'Lady come on! We will give you both a lift.' Another said, 'That is the Christian spirit,' and helped them both onto the truck. They then dropped them off where a relative of the old man lived. Here, too, houses were burning. Mandalay burned for many days and was almost razed to the ground.

Mother managed to contact her friends who took her to live at a doctor's place. Some days later, her friends went to retrieve her things from the trench where she had left them and found all the things intact.

Mother's friends at Mandalay tried to convince her to evacuate to India by plane. Dr George Daniel, a Major in the British army told her how unwise and dangerous it was for a lady to be alone in Burma, and as it was impossible to travel back to our family in Myanaung, she should leave for India. Mother felt in her heart that she could not leave us. The very thought was inconceivable to her but their strong arguments wore her down and after seeking God's guidance, she finally agreed to fly out to India. It was difficult to get a seat with the rush of people but her friends managed to get her name on the list at the airport. Mother wept bitterly. How could she abandon her fatherless children? She prayed hard to make the right decision. While she was praying, people suddenly started crying and shouting in disappointment. Above the din she heard the loud announcement made by Mr Carter that the last plane to take them to India had been shot down by the Japanese and that there would be no more flights. She was so relieved and happy at heart although there was so much panic round her. Women and children too would now have to make the long and dangerous trek across the mountains.

She met a couple at the airport who had been Father's friends and they took her to the home of Mr and Mrs Das who remembered Father with gratitude because he had helped Mr Das get a teaching job. Mother was glad to be with these kind friends as they were planning to stay on in Burma instead of fleeing the country. But they and their nine children were going north to Myitkyina and Mother decided to join them. After a tedious journey on the packed train they reached Myitkyina which looked like a dead city. The people had fled either to India or into the jungles to hide. They looked around for a safe and suitable place and finally chose a Gurkha settlement on the outskirts. They lived here for four-and-a-half months. When Japanese planes circled round the settlement, they would run and hide among the sugarcane plants in the fields. They were safe, although nearby Myitkyina and the airport was heavily bombed. Uncle Dr Solomon, who had also reached Myitkyina, made discreet enquiries and managed to find Mother. He was disguised as a labourer to avoid being forced by the Japanese to treat their wounded soldiers.

Mother was determined to get back to us. Undaunted in the face of danger, she approached the Japanese Lt. General, who was known to be a harsh man, and asked him for permission to travel back to Myanaung. He was the only person who could give her the permit to travel, so she took one of the boys from the settlement with her and went to the Army headquarters. The officers refused her request to meet the Lt. General but she persisted and repeatedly told them it was an urgent matter and they finally allowed her in. The General was seated with two bodyguards standing on either side of him and there was a Japanese flag on his table. Mother was filled with fear when she saw this stern-faced man with slit eyes, frowning at her ferociously. But she plucked up her courage and asked him for permission to travel back to her children. An Anglo-Burmese gentleman who worked as an interpreter there, translated whatever she said into Japanese.

'Sir, I am a widow with four small children below the age of twelve. My youngest child is just two years old. They are at Myanaung in Henzada District. Please allow me to travel back to them by train.' Mother took out a family photograph and placed it before him.

He stared at it for a long time and asked her, 'You

Indian? You Gandhi?' When she nodded, he said, 'Good. Good. Gandhi good man. Small children too far away. Should not be separated from mother. No, no, you go back. Small children should have mother.' He took out a map of Burma and asked her to point to the place she wanted to travel. Then he took a sheet of paper on which he wrote an order that she could travel in whatever mode his soldiers were travelling and that she should not be troubled on the way. He signed the order and put his seal on it. 'You can travel to your children. No one will disturb you.'

This amazing reaction from a man known to be ruthless and hard filled Mother with humble gratitude to her God whom she trusted completely. Everyone at the settlement found it incredible that Mother had the courage to face the General, something none of them would have dared to do.

Two days later she heard that the Lt. General had ordered the Anglo-Burmese interpreter to be shot dead because he was suspected of being a spy. However, the order that she had been given was most effective. Every Japanese soldier she met on the way was extremely good to her and showed her great respect.

Uncle Stephen disguised himself as a coolie, wearing a longyi and a towel wrapped round his head, to accompany Mother on her journey. On the day they were scheduled to leave Myitkyina, they got news that the train station had been bombed in four places and several people had been killed or wounded. However Mother and Uncle were prepared to take risks and postponed their trip by a few days. The Myitkyina–Mandalay railroad was damaged in many places because of bombing by the British. Many bridges too were destroyed so that the Japanese would not be able to follow them to the north. The Japanese needed to use the railroads and bridges, so they used the quickest measures possible to repair the routes; for instance, railway lines were placed on sand-filled jute bags to form bridges and trains had to run on these precarious supports.

On 11 July, 1942, they left Myitkyina. They had to climb into a cattle wagon with thirty-four people crammed in it. They all squatted on the floor and could not move or stretch their legs except when some passengers got off at a station. The train chugged slowly over the makeshift bridges with swirling waters below. It was a tedious, fearful journey and at one point in Sagaing, the train could not cross over Ava Bridge so the passengers alighted and crossed the river to Mandalay by ferry boat. At Mandalay port a cartman recognised Mother and took them into the city. Mother was extremely sad to see Mandalay in ruins. The gates of the palace and some beautiful monasteries were destroyed. The house where we had lived such a happy life had vanished completely and the gates had fallen down. Mother felt her life too was in ruins, but the thought of us renewed her strength and she resolved to find us. A pastor gave them a place to stay in a godown and the next morning they went to the Military Police in charge at the station, to show their papers and were also asked to prove they had taken their inoculation for small-pox and cholera.

After a couple of days they left for Rangoon. All along the way, they saw stations burned down, buildings and whole villages lying in ruins, fields left uncultivated, people and cattle maimed. The land of plenty was scarred and suffering. They were accosted by Japanese soldiers all the way but when they saw the order their stern faces relaxed and one even offered Mother a cup of tea and she shared her biscuits with them. They seemed kind and helpful and well behaved. They gave Mother and Uncle accommodation at the railway quarters and the Indian Muslims who were also living there offered them food. The next day they boarded a train to Prome and from there, the last lap of their journey was along the Irrawaddy River to Myanaung on a sampan, a small country boat. The boat ride was pleasant except when a storm suddenly arose and frightened them. The boat stopped for a night near a village and the next evening Mother and Uncle reached Myanaung. They were so eager to see us and so anxious to know if we were safe too.

Mother enquired of an Indian coolie at the wharf, 'Have you seen an old man, a lady and seven children living here at Myanaung?'

He considered a while and then said, 'Yes Memsahib. I saw them a long time ago. They have now left for India by the land route over the mountains.'

Mother was shocked and devastated. Could such young children have survived the trek? She could not stop crying loudly and saying repeatedly, 'Oh God! How can I live without them?'

Another coolie passing by asked her what the matter was and when she explained to him, he responded, 'I know where they are staying. I carried water for them. Follow me. I will take you to them.'

They could not believe their ears and hurried along with the man who helped carry some of their luggage. Hope and doubt alternated in Mother's mind as they walked along several roads. They entered a small compound and as they stood at the door she was rooted to the spot, unable to move. The scene before her was of her children and nieces sitting lined up on the floor and waiting for me to serve them the hot conjee. Grand-uncle was seated at the table facing the door and it was he who broke the silence. 'Daisy is that really you? Are you a spirit or real? Tell me quickly!' I dropped the bowl of conjee in astonishment and stared unbelieving at my mother who had become so thin and haggard, with her lush black hair changed to white. After the initial shock I ran to hug her and cried out, 'Mummy. My Mummy. You are alive!' I did not care whether she was spirit or real. Soon there was pandemonium and hysterical crying and laughter.

A little later, Uncle Stephen joined us. He too had turned grey and had lost a lot of weight. He embraced his wife and children and Aunty was crying with happiness while the children were screaming and shouting with excitement. Mother hugged and held each one of us tenderly. She could not believe that all this was true! This was the miracle that we had all been praying for and the reunion filled us with such great joy.

Mother believed that God had guided and protected her and given her courage to face all the risks and hardship she had encountered. Her simple and steadfast faith never left her. She often quoted a verse from the Bible, Nahum; 1:7 'The Lord is good, a stronghold in the day of trouble and He knoweth them that trust Him.'

Chapter 6

My Memoirs—Gerry O'Connor

Gerry O'Connor, an Anglo-Indian lady, tells of life in Burma, the effects of the Second World War and the trek to India.

I was the eldest of four siblings born to my parents, Valentine Hugh Antram and Hilda Margaret Antram, née Phillips. I was born in Monywa, Upper Burma but lived most of my growing years in Rangoon till the Second World War broke out with the Japanese invasion of Burma in December 1941.

All the members of our family trekked across the mountains to India. The trek took about one month and we walked many miles, sometimes twenty to thirty miles each day, to reach the next camp to rest. These camps were just bamboo and thatch structures put up by the Ceylon tea planters and the British Red Cross. Food was provided at these camps and we had to leave early each morning to walk to the next camp. There were days when Japanese planes flew low overhead while we trekked, and as we had learnt to recognise the drones of the Jap planes, we used to run under trees to hide from them. The Japs had bombed Imphal which was the next camp for the night, but we had to do a double march to get to another camp—a very tiring night for us refugees. We were not able to carry much luggage and as we became more tired, the burden of our luggage seemed to be getting heavier, so we kept discarding some things on the way. By the time we arrived Calcutta, India, most of us ended up with just the clothes on our backs. Many were ill with malaria and I was one of them. We were sent straight to the hospital.

Later, we were sent to the British Evacuee Camp in Coimbatore, a small town in South India, and stayed there for five years during the war. It was a large camp, run and supervised by the British for evacuees from Malta, Greece, Singapore and Burma. I recall as a teenager that those war years in India were happy times. I guess we were too young to worry about the war going on, and school, dance parties and fun times with friends all seemed exciting. I still have those memories and miss the many friends I made in the Camp. Sadly, some of them have passed away. Many migrated to Australia and when I visited Perth, reunions were organised and it was wonderful to meet my old Camp friends among other friends and relatives.

After the War we were all sent back to our respective countries. My family returned in 1947 to find Rangoon all scarred by the bombings; buildings that were hit and destroyed were still piles of rubble. It took many years to reconstruct and things never got back to the way it was prior to the war. The 'good old times' didn't come back.

On returning to Burma, I finished my high school at St. Mary's Diocesan Girls High School in Rangoon before I began working. I worked for British Airways, then at the

American Embassy and finally at the British Embassy for ten years.

I married William Thomas O'Connor in 1958. His father Thomas Henry O'Connor, an American of Irish descent, had come out to Burma as an oil driller for the British Petroleum Company. He married a Burmese lady, Daw Tu. My husband was the eldest of six children. During the Japanese war, my husband, a sister and younger brother were left behind in Burma while his parents evacuated with the three younger children to Calcutta, India. My husband worked for a Japanese firm in Burma during the Japanese occupation and ironically, that firm later became Mitsubishi, and he continued to work for them for twenty-four years after independence. He passed away of cancer in 1996.

After Burma got its independence on January 4, 1948, the country was caught up with so much internal strife, insurrection among ethnic indigenous groups all wanting autonomous states. The Central Government later became a military government and it was all downhill from then on. Many of the Anglo-Indians and Anglo-Burmese left the country and migrated to England, Australia, India and USA.

Our family finally left for the US in 1977 and I brought my mother with us as my father had died in Rangoon earlier in 1976. We came to reside in Atlanta, Georgia and I joined the British Consulate-General here till I retired in 1993. I got bored as a retiree, so I worked as Administrative Secretary at the Episcopal Church of the Incarnation for eight years. Now, after an illustrious career, I am truly retired and enjoy travelling abroad.

I have visited Burma nine times in recent years to see relatives and friends. Rangoon (now called Yangon) has changed considerably; old buildings have been torn down and high-rise condos and flats have replaced them. There are many new hotels and motels that accommodate the tourists and businessmen who constantly visit Burma, which is good for its economy. However, there is still a lot more that needs to be done, as roads and streets are still in a bad condition. Electricity and water supply are rationed, given on certain days and times to certain areas. I guess this is because the infrastructure cannot keep up with the recent development, the many high-rise buildings and increase in population. Yes, the population of Rangoon has exploded, many from districts and rural areas have come to live in the city for jobs. The traffic is so heavy, mainly with old Toyota cars which run as taxis, and the public buses. One cannot see the roads for these vehicles.

Burma is the land of my birth and upbringing—thus I am bonded to my beloved country. The Burmese people and its ethnic groups are well known for their friendliness, generosity and of course sharing their good food especially with visitors, making them feel very welcome to Burma.

I still cook Burmese food, and I must have my rice and curry every day! Still a Doh Bama. (I am a Burman at heart.)

Chapter 7

War-time Memoirs—
M.P. Vedachalam

This account was written by M.P. Vedachalam and sent to me by his cousin, M.V. Sundaraman from Chennai, who was eight years old when the group made the trek. Both M.P. Vedachalam and M.V. Sunderaman reside in Chennai.

I and my elder brother, Kumar, were studying in the B.E.T. High School, Rangoon in the fifth and seventh standards respectively. We lived at Bauktaw, a suburb of Rangoon and we used to go to school by the suburban train which ran between Rangoon and Mingaladon till the schools closed down in the second week of December. There were a number of Tamilians residing in Bauktaw. On Saturday nights bhajans used to be conducted at Padi Venkatarama Iyer's house. Street bhajans were also conducted during the Tamil month of Margazhi. Life went on peacefully till December 23, 1941. Even on 23rd morning, we had gone to the street bhajan and come home. I was playing pandi (a hopscotch game) with my two brothers when suddenly we felt tremors and saw many aeroplanes flying in the sky. We could also see rocket-like objects shooting across the sky. My mother asked a neighbour what was going on and she replied, 'It is the Japanese. They are bombing Rangoon.'

Immediately my mother gathered us and took us all into the trench that my father had constructed with forethought. We came out after two hours when the sounds of bombing had ceased. There was chaos all over. Those who came in by the train from Rangoon were describing how Rangoon was bombed and how several buildings collapsed before their eyes and how lucky they were to escape with light injuries. The Indians were panicky and decided that the best thing for them would be to leave the country.

The Marghazi bhajans ceased once and for all.

From the first week of January 1942, Japanese planes began night raids on nearby Mingaladon airport. As there was no resistance, they used to come boldly in moonlight and attack the targets. On cloudy nights, they used flares to light up the area. People got used to listening for the sirens and hiding in trenches till the all-clear signal sounded. One night, the sirens came on thrice, so we had to run up and down to the trench and back home. After 3.30 a.m. we fell exhausted on our beds into a deep sleep. In the morning, when Father was preparing to leave for office he suddenly asked, 'Where's Bapu?'

My younger brother was missing! We searched all over the house but he wasn't there. Then we rushed to the trench and there he was, curled up in deep sleep.

One night, we saw red sparks flying from one plane to another and we kids were enjoying the fireworks but our parents dragged us into the trench. After about ten minutes we heard a deafening sound as if a thunderbolt had struck our house. Thankfully, we saw our house intact when we came out of the trench. We later came to know that it was a Japanese plane that had been shot down by a Royal Air Force plane. We went to bed that night thanking God for keeping us safe.

My mother was expecting a baby any day and in mid-January she went into labour. A neighbour took her and my father in his car to the maternity clinic in Rangoon where she had gone for check-ups during her pregnancy. The clinic was locked and the people around the area said the doctor and nurse had left Rangoon. It was an anxious time for my parents, but a kindly neighbour helped with the delivery and all went well. Luckily, for the next seven days there were no air raids. On the eighth night, the siren sounded again and while we were climbing down the stairs into the trench, one step happened to be out of place and my mother tumbled down with the new-born baby in her arms. Miraculously, there were no injuries.

One by one, the Indian families in Bauktaw had begun to leave the place. Before the war broke out in Burma there were regular shipping services between Rangoon and Madras. But in January '42, the services had become irregular. The dates and times of departure were kept a closely guarded secret. Even when the ships were in port, tickets were not easily available. Those who procured tickets through brokers would leave immediately without informing even friends or relatives and in this way several families left for India in January. By February of that year, there were only four or five Indian families in Bauktaw. The previously busy roads were now silent. Sometimes a lorry would come with some local Burmese who would break open locked houses and take away things left behind by the Indians.

On February 16th, my father was informed that there were a few seats left on a ship that was ready for departure, so we hurriedly got ready to leave but on the way we were stopped and told by the occupants of a car coming from the opposite direction that they could not get on the packed ship, so we too turned back. Although this trip did not materialise, we left Bauktaw on 21st February. The British Government of Burma had shifted their headquarters from Rangoon to Maymyo and as my father was an employee of the Burma Secretariat he was told to join duty at Maymyo. At Rangoon Railway Station my father had to show his permit to enter the station. The platform was crowded but we managed to find a few vacant seats on a train to Maymyo. There was no room for a jute bag which contained our cooking vessels so we left it on the platform there. We reached Mandalay the next afternoon and got on another train to Maymyo. When we arrived at Maymyo we found that the town had been bombed that afternoon and all transport had come to a standstill. There were no porters either. All the shops were closed. As we stood shivering in the cold, Father was wondering where to take us. Just then Mr Rajaram, whom we knew, greeted us. He had come to see if any of his friends had come by that train. He offered us accommodation for the night and gave us breakfast the next morning. Father went looking for a house to rent and found that our next door neighbour from Bauktaw, Mr Venugopalan, and his family were staying with some friends. He told my father that we too could go and stay in the big house for a few days.

The course of the war indicated that Maymyo would not be safe for long, so most of the Indian families living there decided to leave for India at the earliest. Father too made plans for our family and about the end of February or beginning of March (I am not sure of the date), we left Maymyo with three other families in our group. We boarded a train to Monywa and after a long wait, the train started on the first leg of our journey. I remember crossing over the Irrawaddy River on the Ava Bridge. The train stopped only at a few places and the local Burmese people welcomed us or waved goodbye to us.

When we reached Monywa, we stayed the night at a rest house and the next morning we got ready to leave by launch. Monywa is situated on the banks of the Chindwin River and steamers plied to and from towns up the river. All passengers were given anti-cholera inoculations before departure. It was nearly 4 p.m. when we finally left. After travelling for about three hours, the launch halted and all of us got down to relax. The ladies lit a fire on the sand bank and cooked the night meal, and after dinner we returned to the launch to sleep. This routine of stopping the journey for the night and starting early next morning with a halt for lunch continued for three days. To break the boredom, the crew would sing some Manipuri songs which still ring in my ear.

On the fourth evening, we reached Kalewa, a small town on the banks of the river. The river was getting shallow so the steamer could not go further. All of us got down and went to spend the night at the house of a local Tamilian. The next day, Father went out and made arrangements for two paddle boats and we got on the first boat and continued our journey up the river during the day, stopping for dinner and to sleep at night.

Two unforgettable events happened on the first night and on the next. While the ladies were cooking food, my father was chatting with Mr Ram, a co-traveller. I was sitting on the riverside and my two brothers were playing higher up on the bank. Suddenly my younger brother, Jeechi, aged two years, slipped and rolled down the embankment into the water. He was almost carried away by the current when Kumar jumped into the river and caught hold of Jeechi's shirt sleeve. The current was strong and he was finding it difficult to hold on, but fortunately Mr Venugopal ran to the water, caught Kumar and pulled them both out. All this took place in a couple of minutes. Mr Ram scolded my father, 'My friend, I am afraid of coming with you. You are indifferent to the safety of your children and are not taking proper care of them.'

Mr Ram did not know what cruel fate awaited him the next night. When the boat halted for the night, we took shelter in an evacuee camp a short distance away. Meanwhile, the other group which had left Kalewa later than us was spending the night at our previous night's halting place. Some of them went down to the river to wash and bathe. Mr Ram's son, Kannu, who was in this group, was sitting on a rock and washing his clothes. One of his garments fell into the water and started drifting away, so Kannu bent down to retrieve it. He lost his balance and fell into the water. He could not swim and the force of the current swept him away to a shoal nearby where he drowned. None of the boatmen could attempt to save him. The news reached our camp the next morning. Mr Ram was shocked and heartbroken. He left our group, boarded a lorry that came that way and returned alone to India.

We continued our journey in two bullock carts which Father managed to hire. But they only took us till the next village where Father had to look for other carts for the next stretch of the journey. It was getting dark and the overseer who was camping in a tent nearby said that it was not safe for us to be by ourselves. So till Father returned, we had to take shelter in his tent. Father came back later to the house he had left us in and panicked when he discovered we were not there. My elder brother heard him calling out his name so he ran to tell him where we were. The next night, we slept in the bullock carts that Father had hired so that we would be ready to go with them early in the morning. It was a caravan of about ten bullock carts. Apart from our group, there were other Tamil families who were also travelling in the caravan. We travelled till about 11 a.m., when the caravan stopped near a small stream. We had our baths and the ladies cooked a simple meal on stones, using twigs for fuel. We resumed our journey till about 7 p.m. when we stopped at a small village. There we had our dinner prepared as in the afternoon and climbed back onto the bullock carts to sleep. This routine continued for the next six days.

Sometimes we had to travel through dense forests where a number of trained elephants dragged logs and timber. The bulls pulling our carts would get alarmed and run as fast as they could if the path got close to the place where the elephants were working. One night, the caravan stopped on the outskirts of a forest and Mother got down, placed the baby on a piece of cloth on the ground and went nearby to do some washing. A big elephant came that way and, seeing the baby, turned and went in a different direction.

On the seventh day, the caravan reached Tamu, a small town close to the Indian border. The journey by bullock cart ended there and we stayed at an evacuee camp for about a week till further arrangements could be made. We had to rest for about five hours in the shade of some trees before we were accommodated in the camp. While we were sitting there, a very tired man who looked like a Manipuri came and lay down a short distance away from us. He seemed to fall asleep, but later we discovered that he had passed away. He was one of the many victims who died of cholera while we were in Tamu. Father made sure that we drank only boiled water and our food too was monitored. The government issued free rations of rice, gram and salt to all the refugees. Mother used to prepare our meals as best as she could with the limited supplies.

Tamu is about fifty miles from the Indian town of Palel. One had to walk across the mountains for two days to reach Palel. The route from Tamu to Palel was reserved for the Europeans and Anglo-Indians. They were provided with elephants to transport them across the mountains and they were also given biscuits and Horlicks. The non-whites, who were mostly Indians, were told to proceed to Myitha, a village twenty miles from Tamu and from there to walk to India by a different route.

Accordingly, we left Tamu for Myitha on the morning of the seventh day since the trek began. The ladies and the younger children were put on the few bullock carts that we managed to get. But the men and big boys, including me, began the walk. We took short rests on the way. Sometime in the afternoon, we reached a fork in the path and one side was blocked by bamboo gates. That was the route that the Europeans were using to get to Palel. It was Indian soil beyond the gate but we were denied the right to use the route. We reached Myitha at about 4.30 p.m. and stayed the night in an evacuee camp. The next day we were given cholera inoculations again. I and some others in the group had dysentery, probably because of the lack of curds, buttermilk and food that we had got used to while growing up. Father got some clarified butter (ghee) from somewhere, mixed it with sugar and gave it to us as medicine. It arrested the dysentery but we were not completely cured. We were anxious to get out of the pace but had to wait six days at Myitha.

At last we began the next stage of our journey. Now all of us had to walk, as the bullock carts could not go up the mountains. Father hired four Manipuris, two to carry our belongings and two to carry one child each on their backs. Father carried Jeechi and Mother carried the two-month-old baby. A short distance from Myitha the path up the mountain began. After climbing for about two hours, we reached a spot where a Gurkha was standing guard with a rifle. Father told us this was the India–Burma border. We crossed onto Indian soil. Although the slope was not steep, we couldn't walk fast and our progress was slow. We were moving in semi-darkness when suddenly we smelt a very bad odour. 'It's a corpse that is rotting,' said the ladies as we all ran past the place.

Father told us all to walk calmly and steadily and we did this for more than an hour in the darkness till we reached a place that had some semblance of human habitation. The

Manipuris who were also our guides told us we could rest there for the night. We all sat down under a tree and Mother wanted to prepare rice porridge (kanji) for us but there was no water to cook with. Our guides told us that water in bamboo poles was being sold by some Burmese nearby, so Father went and bought two five-foot-long bamboo poles filled with water, costing two annas each. After having kanji for dinner, we spread a blanket under a tree and lay down. We fell into a deep sleep almost immediately.

The next morning, we had a cup of coffee each and began walking again at 7 a.m., stopping after about three hours to cook and have lunch. I remember Mother prepared cabbage curry that day. At 2 p.m. we began walking and walking with only a short break to have a cup of coffee. It was made by dissolving coffee tablets in hot water carried in a flask and mixing it with condensed milk from a tin. We came across more corpses on the way. My brother complained that the Manipuri man carrying him was smelly and got down to walk. My other seven-year-old brother was tired and wanted to be carried but the Manipuri porter refused to carry him. When we reached Sitha camp, we had a little rice porridge each and spread our blanket on the ground and slept the night in the open. The guard who had a tent there let Mother and the baby spend the night in his tent. We did not realise that where we were sleeping, spring water was oozing out of the ground till we woke up the next morning to find all the blankets wet.

At about 8.30 a.m., we left Sitha camp. We had to climb a hill and then descend a long serpentine path which seemed to stretch on and on. The forest was dense and we could hear the cry of wild animals. When we saw a rivulet with crystal-clear water we quenched our thirst and, with the advice of our guides, Father went ahead and found a hamlet with some shops. We climbed up a hill to get to the hamlet and we were relieved to get accommodation in a house and stayed the night there, happy to get a meal of puris and sabji from a nearby shop. The next morning, we started walking again, this time on level ground and went past a few villages. When the path joined a highway we saw some army trucks moving along the road. The trucks had been arranged by the Government of India to help the refugees who were trekking from Burma. We stopped a truck, climbed on and said goodbye to our Manipuri guides. At about five that evening, we reached Imphal and spent the night in one of the tents erected for the refugees.

The next morning, a convoy of about twelve trucks was ready to take us and other evacuees on the next lap of our journey. The truck ride was a welcome change and a new experience for us. We travelled for some time on a level road and later traversed up and down several hills on ghat roads. We stopped for lunch and chapattis were provided to us. Then the journey continued across the hills till about 6 p.m. when we reached the rail-head of Dimapur. We stayed at another evacuee camp there and were given free food and railway tickets for our onward journey. The food we were given there made us feel as if we had feasted after a long time. We children were given milk which we had not tasted for nearly a month.

After we had gone to bed Father and Mother discussed their future plans. In the morning we learnt that Father had decided to go back to Maymyo. He felt that if he did not report for duty in Burma when his leave ended on

March 30th, the government in Burma could take action against him as a deserter.

Father made arrangements for our family to travel from Dimapur to Madras by train and for someone to meet us in Madras. He said goodbye to us, sad to go back to Burma but relieved that we were safe in India. Our journey by train was comfortable but we had to get down and cross the Brahmaputra River by steamer and then board another train through the forests of Assam, then through a part of East Bengal (present day Bangladesh) till we reached Parbathipur which was the terminus. So far, we had been travelling for more than twenty-eight hours. While we were waiting at Parbathipur railway station for another train to Calcutta, a Muslim good Samaritan brought us some plates of chappatis and bajhi from a nearby Brahmin vegetarian hotel. He had heard us talking and came to speak to us in Tamil. When we inquired, he told us he was a Congressman from Madras and felt it a duty to help the war refugees. We appreciated his selfless service.

We travelled for about twelve hours on the train to Calcutta and when we arrived at Sealdah, Mrs Venugopal, who knew Calcutta well, took us on a horse-drawn cart to Howrah to catch the Madras-bound train. We got on the train to Waltair where we caught a connecting train to Madras the next morning. Both my brothers were sick, one with dysentery and the other with measles, but at Madras station we got unexpected help from an ex-teacher from Rangoon who had taught my brother at B.E.T. School. He arranged for conveyance to take us to an Evacuee Relief Camp where we were given free food and accommodation.

Next morning, a relative from Monsur came enquiring for us and took us by the morning train to Monsur. There we got down from the train and walked to our great-grandfather's house. People lined up on either side of the street staring at us in disbelief and wondering how we had survived the bombings and other ordeals. We stayed at our great-grandfather's house for three days after which my maternal grandfather and grand-aunt came and took us to Gudiyattam. One chapter of our lives had come to an end.

In the meantime, Father got a lift in an army truck and reached Maymyo in a week's time. Two days after his return, the government decided to shut down their offices in Burma and move to India. Father and other government servants were informed to proceed to India. Thus Father, who had reached Maymyo on April 8, 1942, had to leave for India again one week later. This time he and his colleagues came by a different route across the Naga hills. After enduring severe hardship, he reached Calcutta on May 15th. He had become just skin and bones, but he went from Calcutta to his brother's house in Delhi to join duty in Simla, where the government had set up its headquarters. Another chapter had begun in his life too.

Acknowledgements

Thank You

To the survivors who have said your last farewell: A.J. D'Cruz, Donald Menezes, Thelma Menezes, Gerald D'Souza, Eric Menezes, Kevin Pinto, Doris D'Mello, Patricia Duarte, Especiosa D'Souza, Veronica Carvalho, Hugh Nazareth.

You have passed away, but your memories live on in this book.

Survivors still: Peter Vaz, Isabelle Vaz, Lena Rego, Felicity Fernandes, Albert deSouza, Tony Machado, Wilma Silgardo, Geraldine D'Souza, Renee Pinto, Leo Rego, Sylvia D'Gama.

Your stories made this book possible. I am so grateful to you all.

Arvind Benegal for recording your Uncle Benegal Dinker Rao's fascinating experiences and sending them to me.

Krupa Masoji for allowing me to retell your mother Shakuntala's amazing story and Shyamal Ghosh for sending me the scan of the book, *Bravo Mum*.

M.V. Sunderaman for sending me your cousin M.P. Vedachalam's detailed account of the trek.

Gerry O'Connor for writing down your memoirs and sharing them with me.

Dr Heather Cam DE, Managing Editor and Rights Manager of Newsouth Publishing, Australia for permitting me to use an excerpt from Colin McPhedran's *White Butterflies*.

Jerry Pinto for sharing the story of your mother's family and also of Helen the legend.

I owe you a debt of gratitude for your valuable editorial help and the time you spent to improve my manuscript. Your support and encouragement means a lot to me.

I will always feel deep gratitude for Frederick Noronha. You made the first *Songs of the Survivors* happen and this book has flowed from there.

My grateful thanks to Amitav Ghosh for enriching this book with your foreword and for being a wonderful person in so many ways.

Thank you also for maintaining your blog at www.amitavghosh.com/blog, which is a magnificent resource for anyone interested in the experiences of Burma survivors. It helped me get in touch with Arvind Benegal and Piyal Kundu, and greatly improved the scope of this book.

Thank you Ravi Singh for believing in the book and bringing it to life.

I am grateful to my friends from GoaWriters2, especially Vivek Menezes, Victor Rangel Ribeiro, Jose Lourenco, Vidyadar Gagdil, Isabel SantaRita Vas and Salil Chaturvedi for your genuine interest and concern in the progress of my work and for reading a few chapters of the manuscript initially and putting me on the right track with your observations.

For helping with the maps and pictures, thank you to my brother, Gordon Vaz.

My daughters Shannon and Rachel, my sons-in-law Julian and Nahshon, my brothers Lloyd and Gordon, thank you for being there for me and for giving me the space and time to complete this book. I share the joy of this book with you and I hope my grandchildren, Elijah and Mayah Pinto, will read it some day.

Flickr.com put me in touch with Kelly Wakefield-Betiya (Tresijas) and John Tewell, who magnanimously allowed me to use their photographs of wartime Burma. Piyal Kundu permitted me to use pictures from his collection of Old Indian photographs (gratis). Thank you all so much for responding with kindness to this stranger's request.

Above all else I thank you God for always guiding and taking care of me.

Photo Credits

The publishers and the author gratefully acknowledge each of the photo contributors. The images in this list are identified by their captions.

The photograph of 'Donald Menezes and his sister, Patsy' is courtesy of Lynette Amroliwala.

The photographs of 'Benegal Dinker Rao before the War' and 'Benegal Dinker Rao' are courtesy of Arvind Benegal.

The photograph of 'Gerald D'Souza' is courtesy of Father Coleman D'Souza.

The photographs of 'Evacuation route from Burma showing jeep and elephant' and 'Especiosa D'Souza' are courtesy of Mirna D'Souza.

The photograph of 'A.C. deSouza' is courtesy of himself.

The photographs and scans of 'The Rodrigues family and friends', 'Air travel permit for Mrs Rodrigues', 'Frank Rodrigues' refugee ID' and 'Felicity and Cyril Fernandes on their golden wedding anniversary' are courtesy of Felicity Fernandes.

The photograph of 'Geraldine Pinto's family before the War' is courtesy of Lira Fernandes.

The translation of the Japanese writing on the back of the 'Bombing of Rangoon taken from a Japanese plane' is courtesy of Mustang Koji (on flikr.com).

The photographs of the 'Royal carriage passing through a triumphal arch in Rangoon' and 'Dalhousie Park, Old Rangoon' are courtesy of Piyal Kundu (from www.oldindianphotos.in).

The photograph of 'Lena Rego' is courtesy of Maria Asha Lobo.

The photograph of 'Tony Machado' is courtesy of himself.

The photographs of 'Shakuntala's family before the War' and 'Mrs Shakuntala Peter' are courtesy of Krupa Masoji.

The photograph of 'Eric Menezes' is courtesy of John Menezes.

The photographs of 'AJ D'Cruz before the War', 'Some family members in D'Cruz house' and 'Outside D'Cruz house on 52nd Street, Rangoon' are courtesy of Patsy Menezes.

The photographs of 'Thelma Menezes before the War' and 'Thelma Menezes' are courtesy of Lynn Mudaliar and Oscar Menezes.

The photograph of 'Hugh Nazareth' is courtsey of Noel Nazareth.

The images of 'Japanese invasion money—Rs. 10 note' are courtesy of the National Numismatic Collection, National Museum of American History at the Smithsonian Institution.

The photograph of 'Gerry O'Connor' is courtesy of Clive O'Connor.

Photo Credits

The photographs of 'Sule Pagoda Road, Old Rangoon' 'The Royal Hotel, Rangoon' are courtesy of Asha Pinto and Brian Maung.

The photograph of 'Kevin Pinto's family before the War' is courtesy of Kevin Pinto.

The photograph of 'Geraldine Pinto and her sister, Matty' is courtesy of Sebby Pinto.

The photograph of the 'Bombing of Rangoon taken from a Japanese plane' and of the Japanese writing on its back are courtesy of John Tewell (from Flikr.com).

The photographs of 'Patricia Duarte's family before the War' and 'Patricia Duarte Van Camp' as well as the scans of 'Claim forms for loss of property' are courtesy of Martin Van Camp.

The photographs of 'Veronica Carvalho', 'Isabelle Vaz' and 'Peter Vaz' are courtesy of Gordon Vaz.

The scans of 'Evacuation instructions from Taungyii' and the 'Map showing approximate routes of treks' are courtesy of the Vaz family.

The photographs of the 'Bombed Ava Bridge', 'Old Rangoon from across the river' and the two 'Road signs' are courtesy of Kelly Wakefield-Betiya (Tresijas on Flikr.com). The images were sourced by her grandfather, First Lt. James Wakefield.

The photograph of 'Upper-class Burmese couple' is courtesy of Wikimedia Commons. It was most likely taken by Philip Adolphe Klier in the 1890s.

Bibliography

Aung San Suu Kyi. *Freedom from Fear: And Other Writings.* Revised edition, 2010. Penguin Books: New Delhi.

Brookes, Stephen. *Through the Jungle of Death: A Boy's Escape from Wartime Burma.* 2000. John Wiley and Sons: New York.

Christian, John L. *Burma.* 1945. Collins: New York.

Ghosh, Amitav. *The Glass Palace.* 2000. Penguin India Pvt. Ltd.: New Delhi.

Hall, Harold Fielding. *The Soul of a People.* 1889. https://archive.org/details/soulofpeopl00fiel

Orwell, George. *Burmese Days.* 1934. Penguin Books: London.

McPhedran, Colin. *White Butterflies.* 2002. Pandanus Books: Canberra.

Peter, Shakuntala. *Bravo Mum.* 2004. Writers Workshop: Calcutta.

Pinto, Jerry. *Em and the Big Hoom.* 2012. Aleph Books: New Delhi.

——*Helen: The Life and Times of an H-Bomb.* 2006. Penguin India Pvt. Ltd.: New Delhi.

Shwe Yoe. *The Burman. His Life and Notions.* 1896. W. W. Norton & Co. Inc.: London.

Than Myint-U. *River of Lost Footsteps: Histories of Burma.* 2006. Farrar Straus and Giroux: New York.

Webster, Donovan. *The Burma Road: The Epic Story of the China-Burma-India Theater in World War II.* 2003. Farrar Straus and Giroux: New York.

www.ingramcontent.com/pod-product-compliance
Lightning Source LLC
Chambersburg PA
CBHW061936220426
43662CB00012B/1929